D1171142

Buckminster Fuller. Designing for Mobility

Dedicated to the memory of E.J. Applewhite (1919-2005)

Michael John Gorman

Buckminster Fuller
Designing for Mobility

SKIRA

3 1267 13839 2426

Cover
Shaw botanic gardens, St. Louis,
Missouri

Back cover
R. Buckminster Fuller with his 26 foot
Fly's Eye dome and 1934 Dymaxion Car,
Snowmass, Colorado, 1981

Editor
Luca Molinari

Design
Marcello Francone

Editorial Coordination
Marzia Branca

Editing
Patrizia Masnini

Layout
Paola Ranzini

Image and text credits

Images and writings of R. Buckminster Fuller
Courtesy The Estate of R. Buckminster Fuller.

Unless otherwise indicated, all images appear
courtesy of the R. Buckminster Fuller Papers,
M1090, Dept. of Special Collections, Stanford
University Libraries, Stanford, California.

The vast majority of the photographs in the Fuller
Papers are undated and unsigned, where dates are
known they are given, but in most cases it is not
possible to identify photographers.

First published in Italy in 2005 by
Skira Editore S.p.A.
Palazzo Casati Stampa
via Torino 61
20123 Milano
Italy
www.skira.net

© 2005 Skira editore
© 2005 Michael John Gorman
© 2005 Estate of R. Buckminster Fuller,
Sebastopol, CA
© 2005 Department of Special Collections, Stanford
University Libraries, Stanford, CA
© 2005 Roger Stoller for the illustration
on the back cover

All rights reserved under international
copyright conventions.
No part of this book may be reproduced
or utilized in any form or by any means,
electronic or mechanical, including photocopying,
recording, or any information storage
and retrieval system, without permission
in writing from the publisher.

Printed and bound in Italy. First edition
ISBN 88-7624-265-1

Distributed in North America
by Rizzoli International Publications, Inc.,
300 Park Avenue South, New York,
NY 10010.
Distributed elsewhere in the world
by Thames and Hudson Ltd.,
181A High Holborn, London WC1V 7QX,
United Kingdom.

Acknowledgements

When I began this project I was fortunate enough to have access to the enormous archive of R. Buckminster Fuller now housed in the Department of Special Collections, Stanford University Libraries. I would like to acknowledge the help of my colleagues at Stanford. Jeffrey Schnapp first got me hooked on "Bucky", by inviting me to speak about the Dymaxion car to his seminar at Stanford. Sean Quimby has been a constant source of insights on the archival materials. Roberto Trujillo, Head of the Department of Special Collections has been very supportive of this project within the many Fuller-related initiatives underway at Stanford competing for his attention. The Fuller archive, itself one of his most extraordinary creations, is a 45-ton beast that threatens to engulf all those who come near it, and I had only began to skim the surface before I slipped from its clutches, but I am confident that it will yield very rich pickings to future scholars who, like myself, have not had the benefit of direct access to the man.

I am most grateful to Allegra Fuller-Snyder, Jaime Snyder and John Ferry for the Fuller Estate for their kind support of the project and permission to reproduce images from the Fuller collection and to quote from Fuller's works.

I'd like to thank Kenneth Snelson for fascinating discussions about tensegrity and intellectual property, and for helpful comments on an early draft, Edwin Schlossberg for a wonderfully frank account of collaborating with Fuller, Ed Applewhite for rich insights, gentle irony and secret files, Bonnie DeVarco for sharing her research and deep knowledge of the Fuller archive, Roger Stoller for discussions of his experience of working for Fuller, Allegra Fuller-Snyder for sparkling and invigorating conversations about her father, Theodore Roszak for a critical view of Fuller's appeal to the counterculture, Linda D. Henderson for advice on Fuller's artistic connections and for introducing me to the work of Claude Bragdon, Jay Baldwin for technical advice on Fuller's creations and for keeping the idea of a Garden of Eden alive, Sir Harry Kroto for comments on the naming of Buckminsterfullerene, Maria Gough for suggestions on Ioganson, Ruth Asawa and Albert Lanier for their wonderful stories about Black Mountain College and Don Richter for providing a fascinating first hand account of the creation of the geodesic dome. Their widely divergent interpretations of Fuller have informed this book in many ways.

Contents

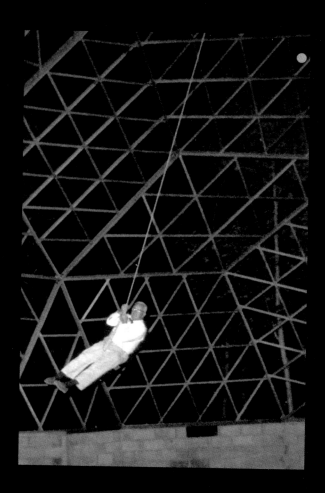

Introduction

"I did not set out to design a house that hung from a pole, or to manufacture a new type of automobile, invent a new system of map projection, develop geodesic domes or Energetic Geometry. I started with the Universe – I could have ended up with a pair of flying slippers"
R. Buckminster Fuller[1]

R. Buckminster Fuller (1895-1983) was not an architect. He never trained as an architect, he vigorously disparaged the architectural profession, and he only received a license to practice as an architect as a token gesture at the age of 79. Yet R. Buckminster Fuller, a.k.a. "Bucky", has arguably done more than any twentieth century architect to challenge our received ideas about building, not as an architect but as a philosopher of shelter. Precisely through not being an architect, Fuller saw the problem of housing as a problem linked to invisible networks of distribution and social organization, as well as to the selection of appropriate materials and building methods.

Fuller's philosophy of shelter was a practical, hands-on philosophy. Its arguments and proofs were encapsulated in performances – public demonstrations of his structural principles – and in built and imagined structures – from the three-wheeled Dymaxion car to the geodesic dome and Cloud-Nine floating cities. "You cannot better the world by simply talking to it", he argued. "Philosophy to be effective must be mechanically applied"[2]. His own career can be viewed as a series of attempts at mechanical application of the fundamental principles he perceived in nature and society.

Where can one go to visit a Fuller building? The question is deceptive. Fuller's buildings were themselves designed to be mobile, to travel by air to any desired plot of land, where they could be moored or anchored. True, there are some Fuller "relics" to be found, from the burned-out skeleton of the Expo '67 dome in Montreal (now known as *La Biosphère*) to the rusted Baton Rouge dome in Louisiana, the Carbondale Illinois dome where Fuller once lived, and, the *Wichita Dymaxion House*, removed from its original location in Kansas and now beautifully re-housed and restored in the Ford Dearborn Museum in Michigan. There are also the Fuller-inspired structures: *Spaceship Earth* in Disney's Epcot Center, a place of pilgrimage for an enormous number of visitors every year, but certainly not a direct translation of Fuller's vision, Nicholas Grimshaw's remarkable Eden Project in Cornwall, the Cold-War radomes once used to house and protect sensitive radar equipment from the harsh climactic conditions on the Distant Early Warning (DEW) Line in Canada and Alaska, the *Octet-Truss* structure present in almost every crane boom, and the geodesic dome atop Salvador Dalí's magnificent memory theatre in Figueres, intended by Dalí as a paradoxical demonstration of the idea that a project doomed to failure is like a building construction that starts with the roof.

Fuller swinging through the geodesic dome restaurant in Wood's Hole, Massachusetts, 1955

Fuller in his dome home, Carbondale,
Illinois

Interior of large Fly's Eye dome

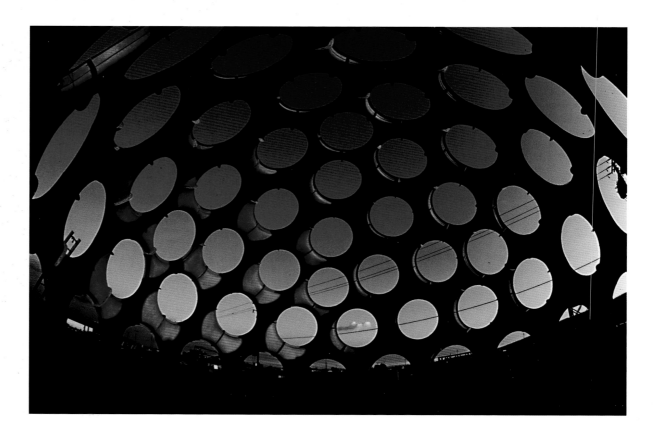

Interior of the Expo '67 dome, Montreal

Fuller's own career is replete with paradoxes. A true apostle of industrialization and mass-production, most of the building projects carried out under his direct supervision were either never completed or were one-offs. What are we to make of this? Even when the conditions appeared favourable for a move into mass-production, Fuller tended instead to move on to the next project, the next philosophical demonstration, often leaving the original project to founder without management. The paradox is removed if we consider Fuller not as an architect, but as a philosopher of building, concerned with the demonstration of truth through performance and modelling more than with dealing with the quotidian concerns of the building industry. Fuller would frequently explain that he worked 50 years in the future, and that his ideas would only be accepted then. If someone works in the future, as any futurist knows, it can actually represent a problem if your ideas start being too successful in the present – the next step would be for them to become commonplace or even *passé*.

For someone who wished for his ideas to be accepted universally, and who believed he was exploring the working principles of nature herself, Fuller was surprisingly concerned with protecting his intellectual property. He was one of few twentieth century figures to patent a cartographic projection, and also patented a geometrical form, the octahedral-tetrahedral truss. Fuller made his students sign forms allowing them to use his new "synergetic" geometry, on condition that any of their discoveries would be his intellectual property. Fuller's approach to intellectual property, an approach that involved him in bitter struggles with many of his disciples and colleagues, again places him outside the traditional realm of working of an architect, but highlights the tensions involved in designing structures using the fundamental principles of nature.

Another paradox resides in Fuller's goal to transform the basic human dwelling. He believed that by transforming people's living environments, you could transform their behaviour. The irony is that Fuller's structures, while enormously successful for certain non-domestic uses, including pavilions for trade-fairs and the protection of radar, were not widely adopted as living spaces, with the exception of a short-lived vogue for geodesic domes amongst hippie communes in the 1970s, an experiment that eventually ended in mass-abandonment.

Fuller believed that, in part through his unconventional assortment of experiences, he had been bestowed with privileged access to the fundamental workings of nature and human society. Paradoxically, he also characterized himself as everyman – "an average healthy human being", in his famous late essay, *Guinea Pig B*, where he reflected on his own life as a grandiose experiment on what one person can achieve when working on behalf of the whole of humanity. Fuller believed that our approach to the problem of the basic single-family dwelling, far from being a low-prestige architectural project, encapsulated an approach to problems of the quality of life of all humankind. For him, the single-family home was a microcosm of the Earth. At the other end of the scale, the tools required to understand principles of architectural structure were also to be found in Nature, but at the very smallest scale of crystals and microorganisms. Fuller did not live to witness the 1985 discovery of *Buckminsterfullerene*, the football-shaped Carbon-60 molecule that earned Sir Harold W. Kroto, Richard E. Smalley and Robert F. Curl, Jr. the 1996 Nobel Prize in Chemistry, but if he had he would have undoubtedly accepted it as independent confirmation of his structural principles. While Fuller's chief admirer amongst professional mathematicians, Arthur Loeb, had stated that Fuller's merit was to introduce 5-fold symmetry into our visual culture, Buckminsterfullerene, or

Interior of the Ford Rotunda Dome,
Dearborn, Michigan, 1953

R. Buckminster Fuller with his 26 foot
Fly's Eye dome and 1934 Dymaxion Car,
Snowmass, Colorado, 1981
Roger Stoller

The 4D Transport, from *Shelter*, vol. 2, no. 5, November 1932

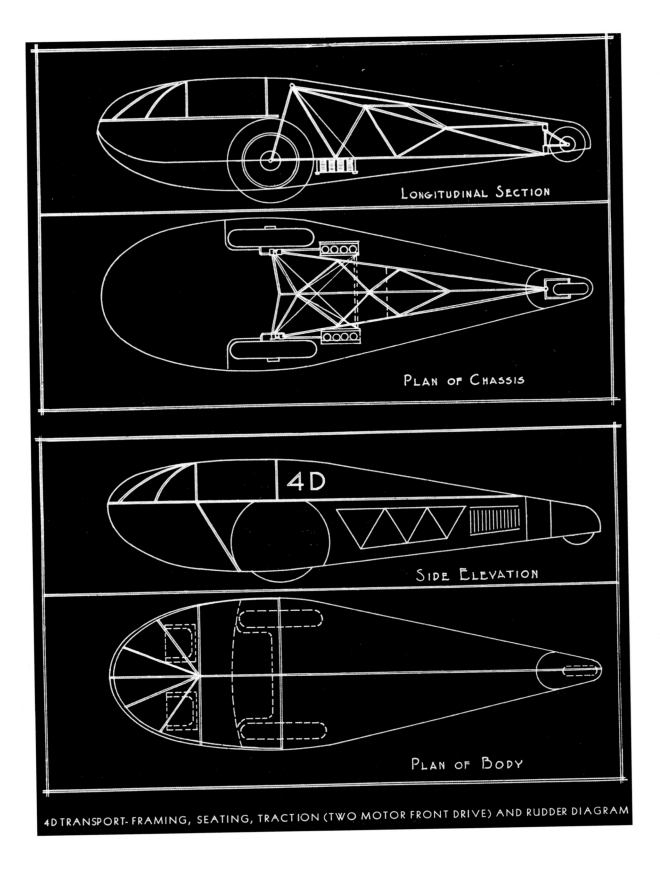

LONGITUDINAL SECTION

PLAN OF CHASSIS

4D

SIDE ELEVATION

PLAN OF BODY

4D TRANSPORT- FRAMING, SEATING, TRACTION (TWO MOTOR FRONT DRIVE) AND RUDDER DIAGRAM

the "Buckyball", as it is now known, demonstrated that nature did, at least occasionally, operate according to Fuller's structural principles on the molecular level.

If Fuller was not at home being described as an architect, he was certainly happy to be called an inventor and to be included in the ranks of his heroes Edison and Bell, not to mention Leonardo da Vinci. In a superficial sense, he received a total of twenty-five U.S. patents, for inventions ranging from his rowing-needles (a catamaran single-person rowing boat) to his Dymaxion bathroom and his "hang-it-all", a suspended bookshelf. In a more profound sense, Fuller was an inventor, and a heroic one, because he believed he had to make a completely fresh start in every cultural field. Rather than attempting to redesign the house, he attempted to redesign the whole housing industry. Instead of considering how to improve conditions in cities, he declared the city itself to be obsolete. Rather than attempting to improve an existing model of automobile, he attempted to address the question of human transportation from first principles, emulating the design principles he observed in nature. Not content with the geometry of Euclid and Descartes, he devised his own "Energetic-Synergetic" geometry. In the heyday of Taylorism, Fuller created his own system of business organization based on the chronological arrangement of documents into a *Chronofile*, inspired by naval logs. Regarding the English language itself as a repository of erroneous notions and muddled thinking, Fuller forged his own distinctive idiom for expressing his ideas, inspired by the density and precision of the telegram. Fuller's linguistic experiments did not end with prose – he was also a prolific and original, if unreadable, poet. Einstein's famous $E=mc^2$ formula was Fuller's model of the economy of poetic expression.

Even more than the inventor, with its connotation of artifice rather than revealed truth, Fuller embraced the persona of the designer. He was most happy to describe himself, and to be described, as a "comprehensive anticipatory design scientist". "Comprehensive" because he was considering design problems in a systematic way, "anticipatory" because he was a sailor, watching the currents of history anxiously to detect long-term trends and help humanity to avoid the shoals, "design scientist" because Fuller saw design not as the cosmetic styling of the Harley Earles and Norman Bel Geddes of the period, but as a science rooted in rigorous principles of economy and efficiency. Fuller steadfastly refused to allow aesthetics to have any driving role in his work: "When I am working on a problem, I never think about beauty [...] but when I have finished, if the solution is not beautiful, I know it is wrong"[3]. While Einstein was the archetypal poet, Fuller saw Henry Ford as the greatest artist of the twentieth century. He claimed that rather than any exterior visual appeal, the most important thing to know about a building was its weight – "The pound is the yardstick by which success and failure are measured" – and he rephrased the problem of the home as a problem of aeronautics – his structures were only temporarily moored to the Earth's surface.[4]

[1] Quoted in Calvin Tomkins, "Profiles in the Outlaw Arena", *The New Yorker*, Jan 8, 1966, pp. 35-97, on p. 74.
[2] R. Buckminster Fuller, *4D Timelock*, Lama Foundation, Corrales, N.M, 1970 (first published 1928), p. 6. Unless otherwise indicated all quotations refer to this edition.
[3] Fuller's reply to a student at MIT about aesthetics in engineering and architecture, quoted by Clifton Fadiman, *The Little, Brown Book of Anecdotes*, Little, Brown & Co., Boston, 1985.
[4] Elaine de Kooning, "Dymaxion Artist", *Art News*, September 1952, republished in Joachim Krausse and Claude Lichtenstein, eds., *Your Private Sky: Discourse*, Lars Müller, Zürich, 2001, pp. 297-301.

Fuller's Rowing Needles, patented in 1970

1. The 1927 Crisis

R. Buckminster Fuller's revolutionary philosophy of shelter was not born gradually, but emerged all-of-a-piece in one extraordinary year, 1927. Where Descartes had created metaphysics anew after falling asleep in a stove-heated room in the Netherlands three centuries previously, Fuller's new philosophy was born of a deep personal crisis. He was 32 years old, bankrupt and jobless. His firstborn child, Alexandra, had died in 1922, in his view due to his inability to provide adequate living conditions for her. The fact that cheap housing, using of the latest materials and technologies was not available for the masses was, for Fuller, a scandal, and the indirect cause of Alexandra's untimely death from influenza, compounded with spinal meningitis and polio. In 1927, Fuller had a new-born daughter, Allegra, to support, and her presence and inspiration is very visible in his early 1928 programmatic sketches in the form of numerous drawings of prams and crawling babies.

According to the most frequently told version of the story, Fuller stood on the banks of Lake Michigan in Chicago, contemplating the waters. On the verge of suicide, it suddenly struck him that his life belonged not to himself, but to the universe. He chose at that moment to embark on what he called "an experiment to discover what the little, penniless, unknown individual might be able to do effectively on behalf of all humanity." Instead of terminating his own life, Fuller thus decided that the responsible act was to commit "egocide", and devote the remainder of his life to improving the lot of humanity. In a different version of the story, also recounted by Fuller, he was walking through the center of Chicago, and as he was going past the Wrigley building he felt himself being lifted off the ground into a sort of sparkling kind of sphere, perhaps a premonition of his weightless geodesic structures. He heard an otherworldly voice speaking to him, as he floated between the Chicago skyscrapers: "From now on you need never await temporal attestation to your thought. You think the truth". After this astonishing revelation, Fuller spent the rest of 1927 in complete silence, working out the details of his new philosophy.[5]

The value of these mysterious accounts of Fuller's primal moment does not reside in their status as documents of historical fact. As myths, propagated by Fuller himself, they "concentrate the truth", to use Hugh Kenner's apt expression. What is undeniable is that 1927 was a fundamental watershed in Fuller's life. Until 1927, he tried his best to conform to traditional New England expectations of a successful career, in the face of formidable financial problems and alcoholism in the prohibitionist Chicago of Al Capone. From 1927 on, divested of the family business, he proclaimed himself to the world at large as a maverick. His problems were no longer personal, they were the world's problems. By committing "egocide" in front of Lake Michigan, a business failure could be transformed into a life-long crusade for the whole of humanity.[6]

The period up to the 1927 watershed is a blur of faded family photographs, anecdotes and pre-

Fuller with wife Anne and daughter Allegra on the banks of Lake Michigan, Chicago, July 1928

Fuller (in foreground) on Bear Island, Maine in 1914

Fuller as communications officer on board the U.S.S. *George Washington*, 1919

monitions: an early childhood hampered by terrible eyesight, hence the coke-bottle glasses, which led Fuller to rely on touch, and to experiment even in kindergarten with building non-rectangular structures that "felt" strong, using toothpicks and dried peas, the idyllic Summer holidays on Bear Island off Maine, where Fuller learned all about boats, about autonomous living, and about tinkering (he made a "mechanical jellyfish", a device like an umbrella used to propel a boat, and created "roll-in-and-pop out" storage cabinets for gramophone records in the family house). Then there were the two expulsions from Harvard: the first, very glamorous, for falling in love with Marilyn Miller, a beautiful dancer, and inviting her whole chorus line to dinner in New York, putting the meal on his family tab, when he should have been sitting exams, the second, less glamorous, for general lack of interest in the Harvard curriculum.

Then there were the mechanical epiphanies. After the first expulsion from Harvard, his family sent him off to work in a cotton-mill in Quebec, where Fuller, with no formal engineering training, developed a deep respect for technology, and a practical understanding of machine parts and metallurgy. Fuller's successes as a machinist were enough to allow him to be invited back to Harvard, but he was far less interested in the formal curriculum there or in an elitist social structure that did not allow him membership, than he had been in the workings of the Canadian cotton mills. Following the second expulsion from Harvard, Fuller worked in one of the least glamorous success-stories of industrialization: meatpacking. Working as a manager in Armour & Co., the largest meat packing company in the world, Fuller resumed his "real lessons" and began to acquire an interest in the large-scale economical patterns of production and distribution. First-hand experience of the "economics of abattoirs, refrigeration, and by-product chemistry" fuelled Fuller's curiosity, as he lugged quarters of beef into export ships and pondered the mysteries of the provisioning of essential goods to the dinner table.

Perhaps most significantly, there was the Navy. In 1917, Fuller volunteered with the family boat, *Wego*, for wartime service with the Navy, and zealously patrolled the coast of Maine. The period he spent in the Naval Academy at Annapolis between 1918 and 1919 was the source of much of Fuller's technical knowledge, and the inspiration for his later preoccupation with what he called "ephemeralization" – the evolution of complex systems towards ever lighter, more efficient and more invisible forms. Naval architecture, Fuller realized, was a triumph of the efficient use of materials. A 10,000 ton "heavy" cruiser car-

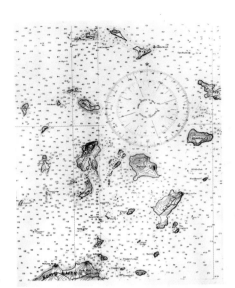

Map of Penobscot Bay (Maine), showing Bear Island, the Fuller's family home

Brochure advertising Stockade building blocks, circa 1923

rying 8-inch guns, a large secondary battery, torpedo tubes and armour plate, in addition to water, fuel, generators, and food for several hundred men, and powerful engines, designed to resist the stress of moving through huge waves, weighed less than one twentieth of a building that had to contain none of these things. The floating microcosm of the naval cruiser, provided with the latest communications and navigational technology, and designed for absolute efficiency provided Fuller with a powerful paradigm that he would use to bludgeon the inefficient state of the housing industry.

For Fuller, the Navy was also a site for experimentation with the latest communications equipment. A ship under Fuller's command, the *Inca*, was the site of the first ship-to-plane voice transmission by Doctor Lee De Forest, inventor of the triode tube. Fuller also invented a "grab-arm" device to rescue pilots who crashed into the sea while attempting to land. Fuller experienced the navy as a "frontier point" of technology, where he had a glimpse of how the technological know-how that went into a submarine could completely transform the quality of life of civilians.

And finally, there was Stockade, Fuller's first ill-starred venture into the building industry. His father-in-law, James Monroe Hewlett, had invented a new kind of building block. Large light blocks, pierced with holes, were piled on top of one another. When concrete was poured through the holes it formed interior columns four inches in diameter. At floors, doors and windows, the columns were tied together horizontally with concrete lintels, forming a continuous concrete framing. The large blocks, which resembled Shredded Wheat, served as insulation, with the concrete columns providing structural support. Fuller experimented with a number of materials for the large blocks, before hitting on excelsior bonded with a binder of magnesium-oxy-chloride cement, formed in a mould under pressure. In spite of producing around 240 houses, the Stockade company was a financial disaster. Hewlett lost his controlling interest and Fuller was fired ingloriously when the company was taken over by Celotex, propelling him to his 1927 crisis.

[5] For the different versions see Fuller, "Guinea Pig B", in *Inventions: The Patented Works of R. Buckminster Fuller*, St. Martin's Press, New York, 1983, pp. VII-XXXII, and Robert Snyder, *Buck-minster Fuller: An Autographical Monologue Scenario*, St. Martin's Press, New York, 1980, p. 35.
[6] Hugh Kenner, *Bucky: A Guided Tour of Buck-* *minster Fuller*, William Morrow, New York, 1973 and Alden Hatch, *Buckminster Fuller: At Home in the Universe*, Crown Publishers, New York, 1974.

TIME LOCK

IN WHICH THE GREAT COMBINATION IS REVEALED IF THOUGHTFULLY FOLLOWED IN THE ORDER SET DOWN; AWAITING THE CLICK AT EACH TURN.

2. Stating the Problem: 4D Timelock

Whether or not R. Buckminster Fuller really spent the remainder of 1927 in complete silence (and the documents for the year in his *Chronofile* suggest that he probably did not), by early 1928 he had in hand the blueprint of a vision for a radically new approach to housing. This blueprint was assembled in the form of a privately published manifesto, *4D*, "written in the throes of mental anguish" which was distributed at the meeting of the American Institute of Architects (AIA) in St. Louis on 17 May 1928, and shortly afterwards, as *4D Timelock*, mailed in 200 mimeographed copies to distinguished thinkers throughout the world. *4D* proclaimed the need for a new kind of architecture, an architecture based on Time, the fourth dimension of Einstein's relativity theory. Fuller himself provided an accurate summary of the book's contents: "The birth of industrially reproduced housing – the inevitable fourth dimension – some pregnant prognostications, and individual duties". Pregnant prognostications indeed – Fuller's manifesto was permeated with a sense of urgency: "No Time Should be Lost Before Reading it, No Time May be Lost in Reading it, No Time Shall be Lost when All have Read it", the book insisted.

The central problem addressed by *4D Timelock* was "the great economic problem of this age and all ages – The Home". Where Le Corbusier had insisted in *Towards a New Architecture* that "the problem of the house has not been stated", Fuller stated the problem forcefully and sketched the outlines of an audacious solution. Le Corbusier's work had been translated into English in 1927, and it undoubtedly had an enormous influence on *4D Timelock*. Fuller acknowledged that he had read Le Corbusier's book while writing *4D*, and even advocated that it should be read as a companion volume, but, characteristically, insisted that his own ideas had been developed completely independently. In his diary for January 30, 1928, he wrote "Called on Russell Walcott and borrowed Le Corbusier's *Towards a New Architecture* [...] RBF read Le Corbusier until very late at night. Startled at coincidence of results arrived at in comparison to Fuller Houses but misses main philosophy of home as against house"[7].

Fuller didn't invent the idea of mass-produced housing – indeed one of his correspondents pointed out that even Leonardo da Vinci had made sketches for prefabricated housing structures. However, Fuller's manifesto for mass-produced housing using the most modern materials also encapsulated the beginnings of a plan for domestic autonomy, which, as Fuller implied, involved a philosophy of the home, not just the house. An intriguing precedent to Fuller's essay is Orson Fowler's 1854 essay proposing a new octagonal home. In this book Fowler, a phrenologist, outlined his vision for the home of the future: "To cheapen and improve human homes, and especially to bring comfortable dwellings within the reach of the poorer classes, is the object of this volume – an object of the highest practical utility to man. It delineates a new mode of inclosing public edifices and private residences, far better, every way, and several hundred

Cover design for *4D Timelock* "in which the great combination is revealed", 1928

26% OF EARTH'S SURFACE IS DRY LAND
85% OF ALL EARTH'S DRY LAND IS HERE SHOWN
86% OF ALL DRY LAND SHOWN IS ABOVE EQUATOR
THE WHOLE OF THE HUMAN FAMILY COULD STAND ON BERMUDA.
ALL CROWDED INTO ENGLAND THEY WOULD HAVE 750 SQ FEET EACH
"UNITED WE STAND, DIVIDED WE FALL" IS CORRECT MENTALLY AND SPIRITUALLY
BUT FALACIOUS PHYSICALY OR MATERIALY.
2,000,000,000. NEW HOMES WILL BE REQUIRED IN NEXT 80 YEARS

RBF
1927

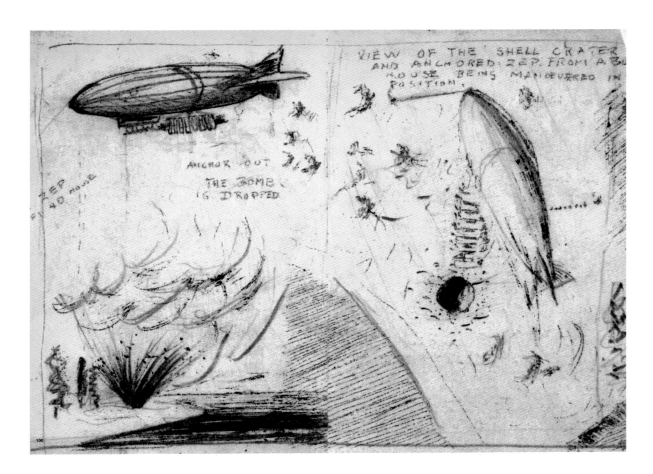

percent, cheaper, than any other; and will enable the poor but ingenious man to erect a comfortable dwelling at a trifling cost, and almost without the aid or cost, as now, of mechanics."[8]

While Fowler's design bears a superficial resemblance to Fuller's in the abandonment of rectangular forms, the similarity ends there – no tension-based structures or industrialized production in Fowler's simple hand-made design.

Like Descartes, R. Buckminster Fuller was keen to argue for the independence of his 4D vision from any contemporary or ancient thinkers. His path was illuminated by the light of revelation and the light of nature, not by the light of any profane authority. Occasionally this heroic pose made Fuller cut a charmingly innocent figure, as when he suggested that he had worked out his own laws of relativity before seeing the work of Einstein, and he was delighted to find Einstein in perfect agreement with him – if Einstein had only chosen not to cloak his meaning behind such obscure language.

Key components of Fuller's solution to the problem of the home were mass production and standardization. Like Le Corbusier, he extolled the principles of design embodied in airplanes, automobiles and ocean-liners. The small house, Fuller claimed, had received none of the benefits of economic pressure that had influenced the design of the airplane and the radio. The housing industry was an absurd throwback to the pre-industrial world. Fuller invited his readers to imagine if, when someone wanted a new automobile, he would invite the designer into his front garden and tell him that the automobile should resemble "the Venetian gondola, a ginrickshaw of the Tang Dynasty, a French Fiacre or a Coronation Coach of Great Britain". The designer would then build the automobile from scratch on the lawn, using pieces of wood and stone. Such a scenario sounded absurd, but was exactly what happened when someone had a house built.

Lightful Houses sketch "Time Exquisite Light", 1928

Patent drawing for 4D house, March 1928

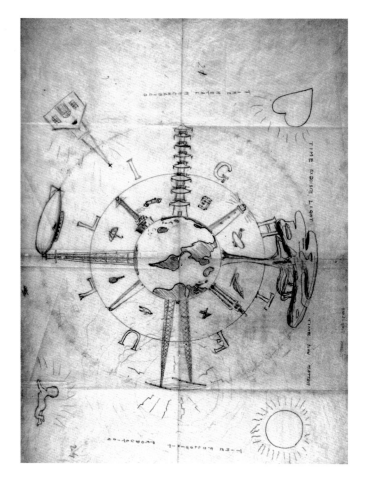

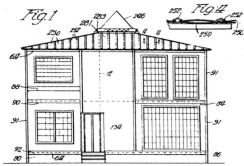

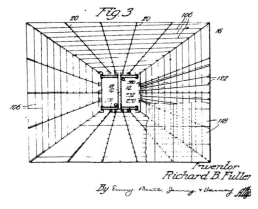

The presence of a modern appliance such as an electric refrigerator in the home was the equivalent of placing a "Rolls Royce engine in a hayrick", according to Fuller.[9]

In advocating mass-produced dwellings, Fuller was also echoing Le Corbusier's mantra: "We must create the mass-production spirit.

The spirit of mass-production houses.

The spirit of living in mass-production houses.

The spirit of conceiving mass-production houses.

If we eliminate from our hearts and minds all dead concepts in regard to the house, and look at the question from a critical and objective point of view, we shall arrive at the "House-machine", the mass-production house, healthy (and morally so too) and beautiful in the same way that the working tools and instruments which accompany our existence are beautiful"[10].

Fuller went a step further than Le Corbusier, though, in actually attempting to turn the "house-machine" into a reality.

"Business of the new 4D house era is going to be damn good fun."[11]

4D Timelock shares a number of key features with *Towards a New Architecture*: both embody a sense of crisis and urgency – Le Corbusier's battle-cry of "architecture or revolution" and Fuller's "No time should be lost", both are pleas for mass-produced housing, both restate the housing problem as a problem of resolving a basic human need for shelter, both endorse decentralization – they are suburbanist fantasies, both praise engineers at the expense of architects, and both incorporate caustic critiques of architectural "style". Fuller was keenly aware that, while in Europe the Bauhaus architects were inspired by the romance

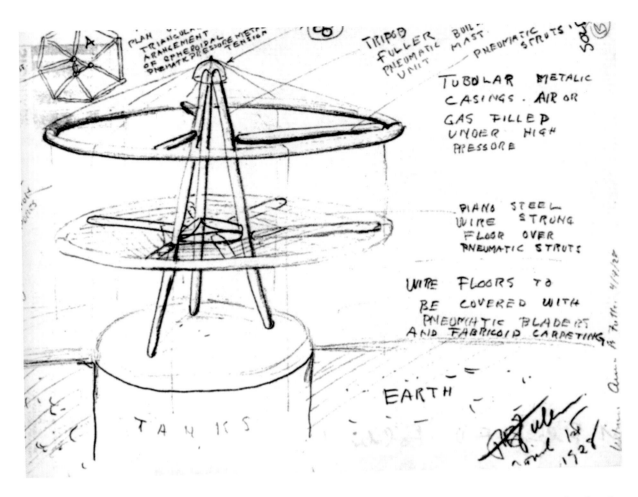

Sketch for centrally-suspended circular
version of 4D house, April 1928

of American industrial architecture, American architects were not developing their own vernacular for the single-family home: "We are in no way creating an architecture of our own (mind you this refers to the small house, not the city building) because we are not being truthful, using our knowledge or daring to create"[12]. Fuller pointed out that the air, road and rail infrastructure in existence in 1928 all pointed towards decentralized human settlement, but "there is no twentieth century home for them to decentralize to"[13].

To Le Corbusier's heady mix, however, we should recognize that Fuller added his own distinctive elements – the Fourth Dimension, or time-based architecture (buildings thought of as temporal entities, rather than just spatial entities), lighter materials, an emphasis on tension as a building principle, direct experience of shipbuilding and aircraft construction as a paradigm for the housing industry, and, perhaps most crucially, air-delivery of housing. Fuller compared the airborne ambitions of *4D* with European Modern in the following memorable formulation: "The ferro-concrete architecture may be likened unto the plastic cocoon of the archaic worm from which will emerge the 4D butterfly"[14]. In appropriating models from ship and aircraft construction, Fuller emphasized the potential of metal as a domestic construction material: "The great new tool of this age is metal from which has been born mechanics or directed mechanical motion, which is governed by fourth dimensional design. It is metal that has made possible centralized production, transportation and distribution through multitudinous channels. Metal has made possible the automobile, the railroad, the airplane, telephone, telegraph, wireless, the clothes on our back and all our foods, and our city skyscraper. Generally and structurally speaking, we use it in our houses in the form of nails only. Structurally the characteristic of the new tool, metal, different from any of the tools of other ages

27

Early design for 4D tower, 1928

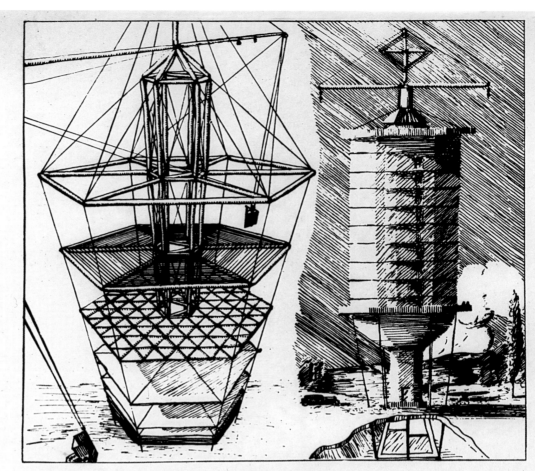

'A LARGER VARIATION OF THE SAME BASIC PRINCIPLE, SHOWING THE CONSTRUCTION DETAILS AND THE APPEARANCE OF A MULTI-STORY HOUSE

is its fibre or tensile strength, tremendously in excess of any other tensile unit ever created"[5].

Fuller quoted financier Roger Babson, who claimed that there was a 3-billion-dollar-a-year business for the producer of the new economical home. Babson, who predicted the stock market crash of 1929, was the author of one of the oddest books of the twentieth century, *Gravity – Our Enemy No. 1*, a vicious attack on gravity, which had caused the tragic death by drowning of his sister ("she was unable to fight gravity"). Fuller also enlisted other unlikely allies for his programme to create the mass-produced home of the future, including Gothic revivalist John Ruskin, who had written "I would have our ordinary dwelling houses built to last and built to be lovely; as rich and full of pleasantness as may be within and without. When we build let us think that we build forever. Let it not be for the present life nor for the present use alone"[6]. Fuller pointed out that Ruskin's description was as applicable to the industrially produced home as to the custom-made dwelling.

In spite of such distinguished support, Fuller's proposal for mass-produced housing did not meet with the support of the American Institute of Architects (AIA), which passed a resolution that the AIA was "on record as inherently opposed to any peas-in-a-pod-like reproducible designs"[7]. It is not clear whether this statement was intended as a direct reaction to Fuller, as, firstly, it was the opening statement of the meeting, and, secondly, it made no direct mention of him – perhaps it was merely a growing concern of the AIA with trends towards standardization.

4D Arctic polar cross station, 1928

4D "Down East". Sketch of rural installation
of 4D towers, circa 1928

Interior view of 4D tower, 1928

Entering a 4D city on the night airway express, 1928

Daytime view of 4D city with Zeppelin, 1928

"Education and the proper upbringing of the young in modern, truthful, healthful environment will quickly efface crime and both mental and physical deformities."[13]

Nonetheless, Fuller reacted vigorously in the version of the manifesto that he mailed out to distinguished thinkers after the St. Louis meeting: "Is it not the truth of standardization that ever pours more individual freedom and happiness into life?" he asked his readers. In response to the equation of standardization with monotony, he countered with arguments tinged with a touch of contemporary eugenics: "If anyone was forced to wear a different kind of shoe altogether from other people, it would be almost surely a sign of some deformity, not a sign of mental or spiritual individuality. The same will soon be true of a house". Moreover "deformities of post or ante-birth are most attributable to filth, ignorance, slovenliness, which in turn are directly attributable to improper facilities and drudgery in the home".

Fuller's vision was sketched in a series of extraordinary mimeographed drawings contemporary to the book. Perhaps the most radical suggestion was the means of distribution of his mass-produced houses. A Zeppelin would drop a bomb on a desired site, producing a large crater. The same Zeppelin would then drop a ten-deck 4D tower neatly into the crater, to be fixed into place by pouring cement.

Fuller's *Lightful Towers* – both lightweight and light-gathering were designed to be hexagonal modular structures built around a central chassis, and capable of vertical extension by means of a roof-mounted crane. People would travel to and from their 4D homes by means of small teardrop-shaped planes capable of prolonged ground-taxiing. There is a sense of kinship between Fuller's striking mimeographed drawings of 4D cities, and streets lined with ten-deck towers and another contemporaneous piece of paper architecture, Georgii Krutikov's 1928 plan for a *Flying City*. Unlike Fuller's ten-deck towers, which were merely meant to be flown into place, Krutikov's futuristic six-deck towers were kept airborne above the

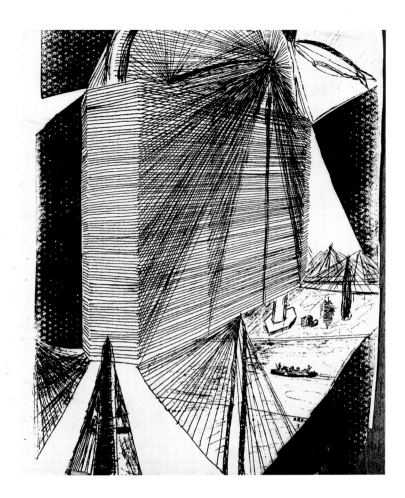

earth's surface on flying rings with the aid of nuclear energy. Their citizens could fly between them by means of a teardrop shaped "flying cabin". Krutikov's project, which Fuller could not have known about when he was preparing *4D Timelock*, was light on technical details, but demonstrates that the idea of buildings travelling through the air was also animating the young artists and architects at the Vkhutemas in Moscow.

Convinced that his plan for mass-produced housing would render city-dwellings obsolete, Fuller believed that island dwellings, like his own beloved Bear Island, would become increasingly attractive, and even wrote to his mother to suggest that the value of island property would be radically increased once his ideas took effect. He advised his mother to sell their house in Cambridge, Massachusetts immediately, as the price of urban real estate was bound to fall dramatically: "If the rest of the family want to keep their money in land, I should recommend transferring the money for the sale of the Cambridge property to the purchase of additional islands, picked for their landing facilities. In a year or so, when my 4D houses are ready, we will be able to put them up on the islands in one day, with every facility of modern city luxury built in, quite as comfortable in winter as any other time, on the installment plan, for a dollar down... There is no question that what I have predicted will come about"[19].

Fuller's proposed buildings were intended to be "drudgery proof" homes. The latest modern appliances would free-up valuable time for leisure activities and self-improvement. Children, living in their 4D Towers in "Labrador, the tropics or the orient", would be able to spontaneously educate themselves by tuning into televisions (televisions, in 1928!) with lectures given by the President of Harvard, the Professor

Goodrich airship moored to 4D tower, 1928

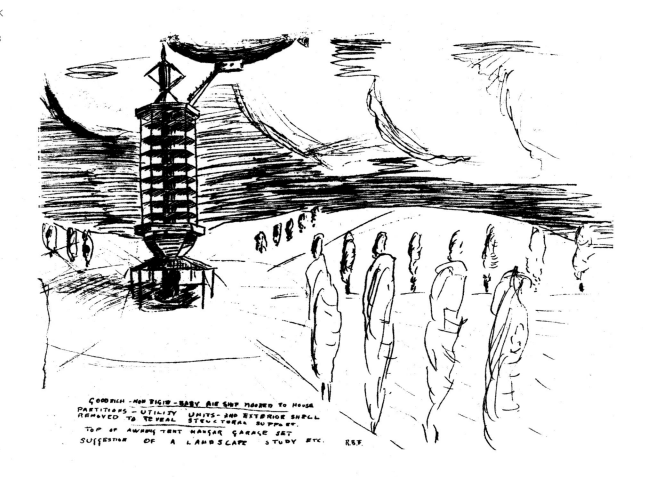

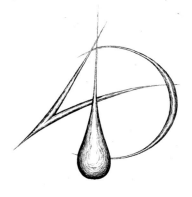

4D logo, combining compass-needle,
teardrop and crescent moon, 1928

of Mathematics at Oxford, or the doctor of Indian antiquities at Delhi. Fuller's 4D Towers, and later Dymaxion Houses, were designed to be very bouncy. Pneumatic beds were provided, and even the floors were made of pneumatic layers placed over steel tension wires, so the sensation of walking around was similar to walking on a football. All doors in Fuller's 4D homes were to be overhead roller doors, inflatable doors, or revolving doors, to prevent dust. Natural light would be enhanced by strategically placed mirrors, artificial light would be indirect and controllable by dimmer switches. The 4D House would be erectable in one day, complete with every modern labour-saving device available, and would be similar to a vertical ocean liner. It would include an electric-vacuum range to cook the perfect steak and the clothing worn by the happy inhabitants would not require ironing.

Why "4D" though? As I understand it, Fuller's appropriation of the Fourth Dimension has a number of levels. At the lowest level, his houses were marked off in "time units" radially from the chassis. At the highest level, his 4D houses were designed to save time for leisure, and release people from servitude to poor architecture. In addition to Einstein, Fuller was an avid reader of the work of Claude Bragdon, whose writings, including *Architecture and Democracy* and *Four-Dimensional Vistas*, did much to popularize the idea of the Fourth Dimension. Bragdon's fourth dimension was an additional spatial dimension, however, not the spatial representation of time that so intrigued Fuller.[20] Fuller also introduced the central idea of mobility into home ownership – revising existing customs of land tenure and financing housing, and perhaps paving the way for that most American of suburban utopias, the trailer-park.

The patent drawings that were produced in March 1928 to accompany *4D Timelock* were signif-

Early sketch of 4D tower home, including pool, gymnasium, grill, music and dancing areas at lower floors, 1928

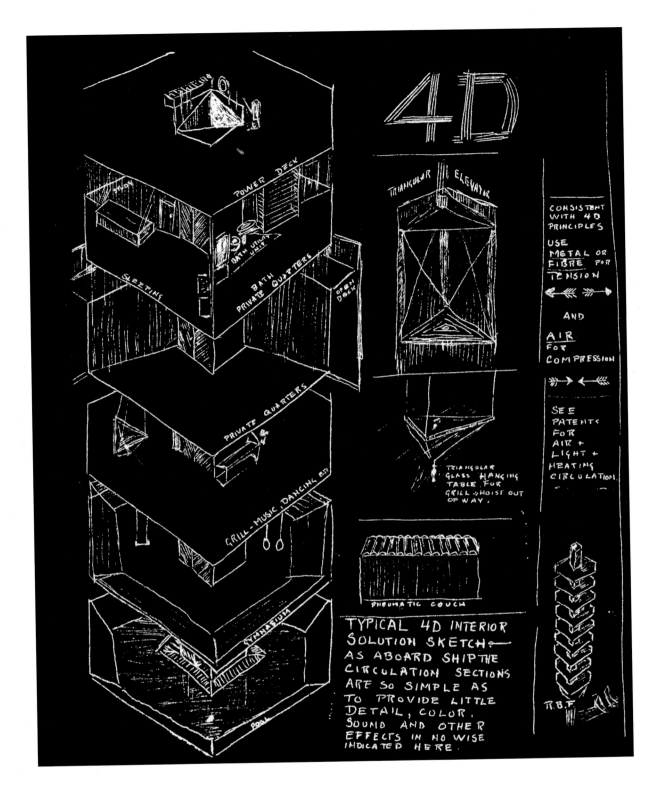

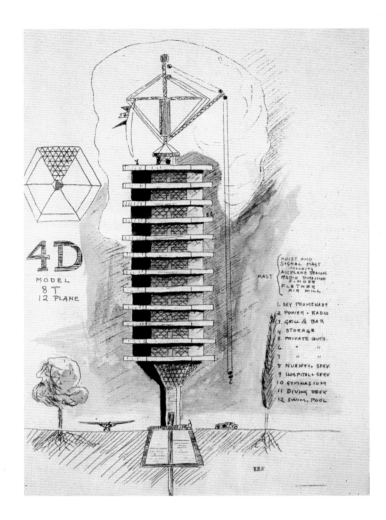

icantly more conservative than Fuller's 1928 sketches of his 4D Towers. The house that they depicted was rectangular – according to Fuller because his patent attorney felt that this would be more palatable to the patent examiners. Nonetheless, like the 4D lightful towers it was built around a central chassis, or "central nervous system" as Fuller called it, and incorporated the tension-based construction principles of the 4D Towers. Fuller disliked the drawings from the rejected patent application, describing them as looking like "pictures of a man with but one foot and one toe on that foot". It is possible that Fuller's ideas developed rapidly from an initial rectangular "Fuller house" in March 1928 to a circular model resembling a bicycle wheel, and finally to a hexagonal model, that had the great benefit of allowing the forces on the central chassis to abate symmetrically, in April 1928. The Barnes-Wallis airship landing-pylon, depicted in some of the 4D drawings, appears to have been influential on his design for the central chassis. Fuller's 4D Towers were intended as an example of what he described as "building from the inside out". They were intended to be planted in the ground, like trees, suspended from a central mast, and in late 1928 Fuller described his 4D Tower as "a synthesis of the American skyscraper, the oriental hexagonal pagoda, with the structural strength of a super-dreadnought, and the lightness and delicacy of the finest of the oriental domestic design"[21].

Were Fuller's early designs influenced by other architects? In a 1955 essay entitled *Influences on my Work*, he answered emphatically in the negative: "Many people have asked if the Bauhaus ideas and techniques have had any formative influence on my work. I must answer vigorously that they have not".

4D city by night, circa 1928

12 deck 4D tower, 1928.
The designation "8T" refers to the eight
yards from the centre to the periphery,
understood as units of time.

Sketch of 4D tower installation for 1929
Chicago Home exhibition

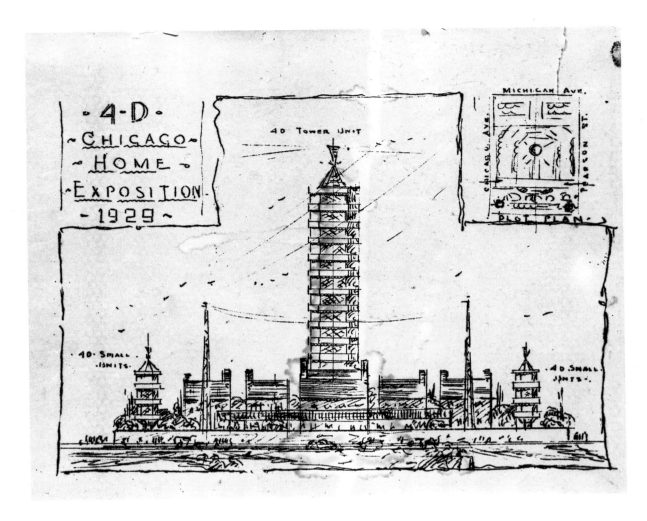

Instead, he argued, his own unique series of formative mechanical experiences, from the cotton mill to the Navy, were responsible for his approach to design.[22] The *Dymaxion Chronofile*, Fuller's enormous chronologically organized personal archive, suggests a more complex picture. It suggests that between 1927 and 1928, Fuller was not just incubating his vision, but reading voraciously about the work of Le Corbusier, Mies van der Rohe, Walter Gropius, and the Russian Constructivists, especially Alexander Vesnin. Photographs from Badovici's magazine *L'Architecture Vivante*, containing photographs of Mies van der Rohe's Chicago Tribune Tower model, and the project for the Moscow Palace of Labour by the Vesnin brothers, with its characteristic tension masts, are present in the *Chronofile* for 1928. The same volume contains a hand-written list of sources that Fuller had consulted in preparing his *4D Timelock*, including the main architectural organs of the day, that challenges Fuller's romanticized account of his prophetic vision born of hands-on experience alone.

Nonetheless, we should recognize that Fuller had serious criticisms of the proponents of the International Style. He felt that in their buildings, Walter Gropius, Mies van der Rohe and Le Corbusier were using industrial lines as a cosmetic varnish on buildings that remained essentially hand-made, and embracing the aesthetic of machine-production, rather than performing a true industrialization of the housing industry. Fuller's "doing more with less", a principle of economy, is not to be equated with Mies van der Rohe's "less is more", primarily an aesthetic position.

Although undoubtedly a raw piece of writing, and full of the heady optimism in technological

4D tower seen from below, circa 1928

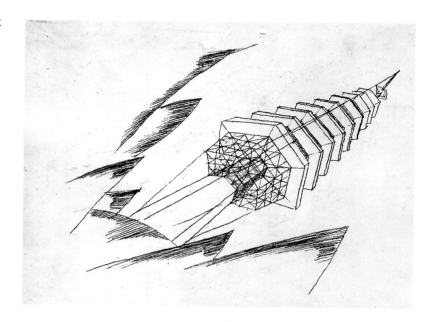

progress that preceded the 1929 stock market crash, Fuller's *4D Timelock* contained the germs of many of his lifelong projects: the use of tension as a building principle, mass-production, standardization, decentralization, autonomous living, air-delivery, the use of lightweight alloys in construction, hexagonal symmetry, education reform, and the house as environmental control.

Air-delivery of housing was perhaps the single most innovative element of Fuller's proposal. Often overlooked as a mere eccentricity or a historical anomaly of the Zeppelin age, air-delivery was responsible for many of the central principles of Fuller's approach to design. The logic behind air-delivery, when articulated, is powerful and surprisingly simple. Contrary to some interpretations, Fuller's lifelong ambition was not to deliver pre-fabricated building components for on-site assembly by hand. It was to deliver complete, mass-produced homes, as one would deliver a new car.

Delivery by rail or road would necessarily limit the width of a pre-assembled home through the need to pass through tunnels and under bridges. Delivery by ship was a viable solution only for coastal areas and inland waterways. Only air-delivery promised the possibility of placing an industrially built home at any point on the Earth's surface, including the North Pole, and did not put *a priori* limitations on the dimensions of the house. Unlike traditional forms of delivery, air-delivery of complete houses did imply strict limitations on the weight of a completed building, even using the largest airships available.

This goal, I want to suggest, was the oxygen that nourished Fuller's lifelong obsession with reducing the weight of buildings – something that had not previously been a central concern for architects. The goal of producing lighter buildings led Fuller to the analysis of structures based on tension, rather than compression. The tensile strength of metals, per unit weight, far exceeded the compressional strength of any known material per unit weight, so, given that the task at hand was to make air-deliverable buildings, tension appeared to be the most promising approach.

This was also why Fuller suggested that any structures that were to be subject to compression in his houses should be inflatable/pneumatic, for example the beds and floors. Structures based on tension rather than compression (piling bricks and mortar on top of one another) led Fuller to experiment with radial symmetry in his structures. It is difficult to distribute forces evenly in a suspended rectangular floor,

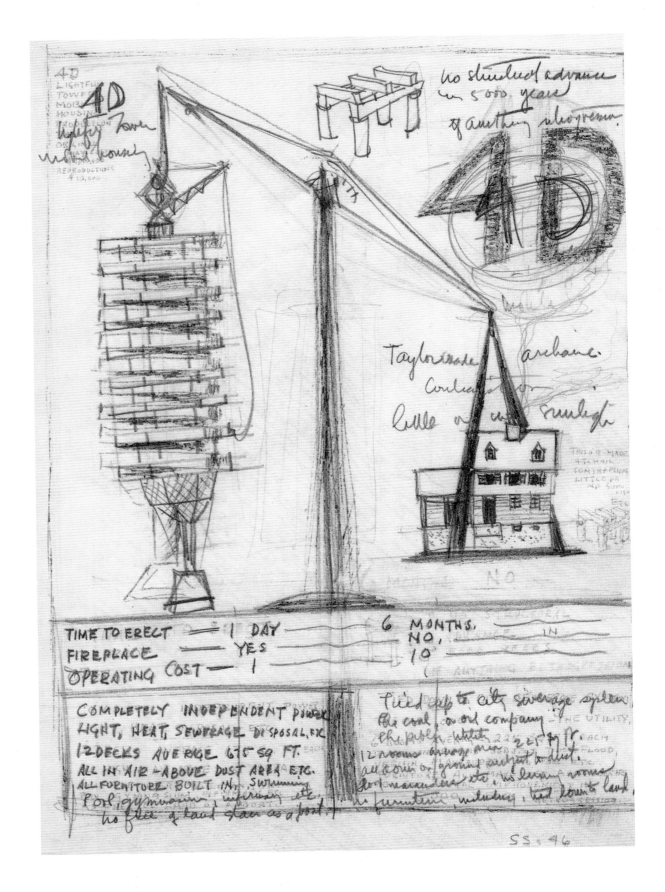

Comparison of Lightful Houses
and traditional homes, 1928

Fuller witnessing the "first airlift of man-useable shelter in history", a Sikorsky helicopter lifting a geodesic dome, Raleigh North Carolina, 1954

hence the awkward cantilevering in the original 4D patent drawings. A circular or hexagonal floor allows forces to be distributed evenly. A hexagonal floor has the added advantage of being composed of six equilateral triangles, implying equal-length radial and circumferential struts. So, from giving himself a simple design problem: the delivery of industrially produced housing to any point on the Earth's surface, Fuller derived both tension-based architecture and hexagonal symmetry. In 1928 Fuller was still thinking of axially symmetric buildings – horizontal floors hanging from a vertical central mast. It was only later, through an intense exploration of geometry of the sphere that he began investigating structures with multiple planes of symmetry.

In 1928, the year of the maiden-voyage of Hugo Eckener's Graf Zeppelin, airships appeared to have a dazzling future. The disastrous explosion of the *Hindenburg* in 1937 ended the golden age of the dirigible and put Fuller's dream of airborne buildings beyond reach, at least for the moment. In 1954, Fuller's objective was proved to be possible, as a U.S. Marines' Sikorski helicopter lifted a geodesic dome. Fuller proudly inscribed the back of the photograph of this event with the following note: "First airlift of man-useable shelter in history. Airlifts have been made possible by the gradual but orderly evolution of Mr. Fuller's search, research and development initiated in Chicago in 1927, which set about in 1927 to find means of developing shelter of such high performance per pounds of invested resource that structures could be delivered by air and thus avoid the needle's eye dimensions of grounded traffic and their plurality of frustrating and uneconomic exigencies. If airlifted, they could enjoy complete assembly in jigs at preferred economic force and under all the attendant effectiveness and economy that have for centuries characterized the science and art of ship building – first for the liquid and second for the air-ocean launchings. R. B. Fuller in foreground".

Fuller's buildings, in 1954 as in 1928, were always intended to fly – this emotional moment in Raleigh, North Carolina was his first successful take-off, and a tribute to his remarkable tenacity. Without large airships, Fuller's ambitious objective of air-delivering factory-produced multi-family homes complete with all fixtures and fittings has remained elusively out of reach, but the logic behind this goal is as impeccable now as it was in 1928.

[7] *Dymaxion Chronofile*, 1927-28, Stanford University Libraries, Department of Special Collections, R. Buckminster Fuller Papers, M1090, Series 2, Box 16, Vol. 30, quoted in Loretta Lorance, "Buckminster Fuller – Dialogue with Modernism", *PART*, vol. 7, http:// dsc.gc.cuny.edu /part/part7/articles/loranc.html.
[8] Orson S. Fowler, *A Home for All, or The Gravel Wall and Octagon Mode of Building*, Fowlers and Wells, New York, 1854, discussed in H. Ward Jandl, *Yesterday's Houses of Tomorrow: Innovative American Homes 1850 to 1950*, The Preservation Press, Washington D.C., 1991.
[9] Fuller, *4D Timelock*, cit., p. 4.
[10] Le Corbusier, *Towards a New Architecture* (Vers

une architecture), translated from the 13th French edition, with an introduction by Frederick Etchells, Payson & Clarke, ltd., New York, 1927, p. 12. All quotations refer to this edition.
[11] Fuller, *4D Timelock*, cit., p. 35.
[12] Fuller, *4D Timelock*, cit., p. 3.
[13] Fuller, *4D Timelock*, cit., p. 12.
[14] Letter to Rosamond Fuller, August 11, 1928, in Fuller, *4D Timelock*, cit., p. 78.
[15] Fuller, *4D Timelock*, cit., p. 4.
[16] Ruskin, *Seven Lamps of Architecture – The Lamp of Memory*, quoted in Fuller, *4D Timelock*, cit., p. 1.
[17] "Cities Becoming 'Peas of One Pod', Architects Warn", *St. Louis Star*, May 17, 1928. This

article makes no mention of Fuller or 4D.
[18] Fuller, *4D Timelock*, cit., p. 6.
[19] Fuller to his mother, Caroline W. Fuller, July 16, 1928, in *4D Timelock*, cit., p. 73.
[20] On Bragdon, see Linda D. Henderson, *The Fourth Dimension and Non-Euclidean Geometry in Modern Art*, Princeton University Press, Princeton, 1983.
[21] R. Buckminster Fuller, "Tree-Like Style of Dwelling is Planned", *Chicago Evening Post*, December 18, 1928.
[22] "Influences on My Work (1955)" in Krausse and Lichtenstein, eds., *Your Private Sky Discourse*, cit., pp. 49-61.

3. The Dymaxion House

Reactions to the self-published manuscript of *4D Timelock* varied widely. Avery Pierce heralded Fuller as finally bringing H.G. Wells' utopian fantasies within reach. Physicians wrote to Fuller to endorse his view that the birth of "undesirables" was due to poor housing. Deformity was, yet again, pitted against standardization. The famous advertising executive Bruce Barton was curtly dismissive, echoing Fuller's own critique of Einstein: "Possibly there is something in Mr. Fuller's idea, but it is so well concealed in his language that I have not discovered it"[23].

Nonetheless, Fuller had sufficient faith in his vision to proceed with designing a prototype 4D House. His prototype underwent a complex evolution. First, there were the drawings of a rectangular house from the rejected patent application prepared in March 1928. Then, in April 1928, there appears to have been a brief flirtation with a circular structure of tubular metal casings filled with pressurized gas and suspended from a central tripod. The precise moment when Fuller hit upon the hexagon is difficult to determine (an early sketch even includes a rough seven-sided plan). The 4D Towers, which appear to date from around April 1928, are hexagonal, as was the sketch for the 4D House that he presented at Le Petit Gourmet Restaurant in Chicago in September 1928. Hexagonal symmetry, presumably hit upon as a practical solution to even weight distribution in structures hanging from a central mast, was to become a driving concern for Fuller, and one that would bring him along an interesting path of geometrical exploration.

When he moved to making demonstration models for his 4D House, Fuller began with a simple structural model – two load-bearing hexagons suspended rather loosely from a central tripod-mast. In 1929, with the aid of design students in Chicago, he moved on to a second paper model, which demonstrated the different functions of the different parts of the one-storey hexagonal house, including the living spaces, tanks and parking spaces beneath the house, and even a futuristic teardrop-shaped vehicle and a small plane for transportation of the inhabitants, brought up to the main house by a triangular elevator in the central mast.

This model of the 4D House was the centerpiece of an interior furniture display at the Marshall Fields Department Store in Chicago in April 1929. In leading up to the launch, Waldo Warren, the ad-man who had coined the word "radio", pointed out that "4D" sounded like an apartment number. After a long one-way conversation with Fuller, he picked out the key words "dynamic", "maximum" and "ion" (or "tension") and the word *Dymaxion* was born.

What kind of furniture did Fuller imagine in the new industrially produced home? He drew sketches of a suspended glass table, anchored with wires illuminated by neon tubes to prevent collisions and a translucent air couch, suggesting that the furniture of the new home should resemble acrobatic equipment.

First (structural) Dymaxion House model, 1929

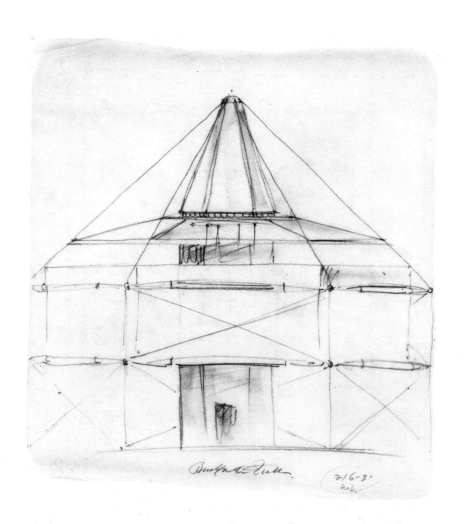

When he presented the *Dymaxion House* model at the Harvard Society for Contemporary Art in May 1929, he gave a description of the materials employed. The walls, windows and ceilings would be made of Casein, "a translucent opaque [sic] sheeting made from vegetable refuse". The bathrooms would be cast in a single sculptural unit of Casein, the doors would be made from silver balloon silk, and would be inflatable, thus dust-proof, the shelter-covers would be made from Duralumin, the floors would be "inflatable rubberoid units". A single integral assembly would consist of desk, filing-cabinet, typewriter, calculating machine, telephone, radio-television receiver, dictaphone, phonograph and safe. As for lighting and heating, an oil engine would both warm the house and illuminate it "by a system of mirrors through the translucent walls". The mast housed lenses to concentrate the heat and light of the sun and divert them to where they were needed. The house was designed, according to Fuller, as a machine in which to live, which eliminated "Drudgery, Selfishness, Exploitation, Politics and Centralized Control", while saving time for "Education, Amusement, and Advancement"[24].

The house even had a "go ahead with life room", designed for spontaneous intellectual exploration, where children could develop self-education on a selective basis, through built-in radio, television, maps, globes, "O-volving" bookshelves, drawing boards and typewriters, so that they could encounter others as "real individuals and not "crowd non-entities". Intellectual autonomy was as much a component of Fuller's home as autonomy with respect to basic human needs. Indeed, in Fuller's radical design, spontaneous intellectual development was recognized as a basic human need, and in many ways his Dymaxion

Sketch of Dymaxion House, 1929

Third Dymaxion House model, 1929

Second Dymaxion House model, 1929

Third Dymaxion House model, 1929. The
nude female figure demonstrates the
perfect climate control of the house

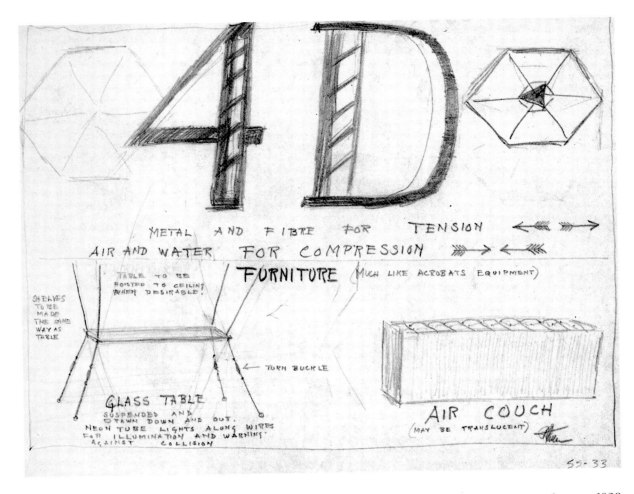

House was the physically manifested antidote to everything that Fuller had battled against in his pre-1928 years. He would later describe the Dymaxion House as "designed to withstand all forces which seek to penetrate or destroy human life process".

Launched on a circuit of lectures, Fuller moved to New York in autumn 1929. During this period, while moulding his public self, Fuller experimented sartorially. Initially, he dressed in a T-shirt, khaki trousers and running shoes, anticipating the "business casual" look of late twentieth century California, but his unusual clothing attracted too much attention, so he quickly resolved to "be invisible", by dressing in a black suit and tie, like a bank clerk, to ensure that his audience concentrated on the message, rather than his personal eccentricity. His wife and daughter lived in Long Island, but he stayed in Greenwich Village, drinking heavily and discovered an intoxicating world of artists and intellectuals.

In the studio of sculptor Antonio Salemme, Fuller created a new, metal model of the Dymaxion House including a nude woman lying on the bed, like an exotic bird inside an aluminium cage. Ostensibly, this was a demonstration of the perfect climate control that removed the need for bedclothes. In Romany Marie's, a Bohemian restaurant in the Village, Fuller gave lectures about his Dymaxion House. It was there that he encountered sculptor Isamu Noguchi, fresh from studying with Brancusi in Paris. Noguchi, later to become a lifelong friend, was fascinated by "Mr. Fuller", as he called him, and offered to sculpt his portrait. Noguchi was exploring the use of materials that did not permit shadows, and thus challenged the traditional idea of using shadow to produce definition. At Fuller's suggestion, Noguchi plated the bronze bust he made of Fuller with the same chrome, nickel and steel alloy that Henry Ford had just used on the radiator grilles of the Model A car, "form without shadow" and an important early example of the use of industrial materials in art. Under Fuller's influence Noguchi also painted his whole studio in aluminium paint, so that "one was almost dazzled by the lack of shadows"[25].

During this exuberant period, Fuller also painted Romany Marie's tavern with aluminum paint, and redesigned the interior on the principle that "a room should not be fixed, should not create a static mood, but should lend itself to change so that its occupants may play upon it as they would upon a piano". In a time of material poverty and expanding mental horizons Fuller discovered artists to be fellow travellers. "I feel that it is the artists who have kept the integrity of childhood alive until we reach the bridge between the arts and sciences", he later wrote. Artists were the only people who weren't blinkered by over-specialization. "I didn't seek artists but I found myself years ago befriended by artists, not just as painters, but dancers, sculptors and artists in general". The Greenwich Village artistic *demi-monde* of the late 1920s and early 1930s was a mind-expanding antidote to Fuller's stern, parsimonious New England upbringing.

[23] Bruce Barton to L.J. Stoddard, June 8, 1928, in *4D Timelock*, cit., p. 50.
[24] "Harvard Society of Contemporary Art Catalog – 4D" in Fuller, *50 Years of the Design Science Revolution and the World Game*, Southern Illinois University, Carbondale, 1969, pp. 5-14.
[25] Isamu Noguchi quoted in Krausse, Joachim and Claude Lichtenstein, eds., *Your Private Sky: R. Buckminster Fuller The Art of Design Science*, Lars Müller, Zürich, 1999, p. 150.

Poster for exhibition of Dymaxion House, Harvard University, 1929

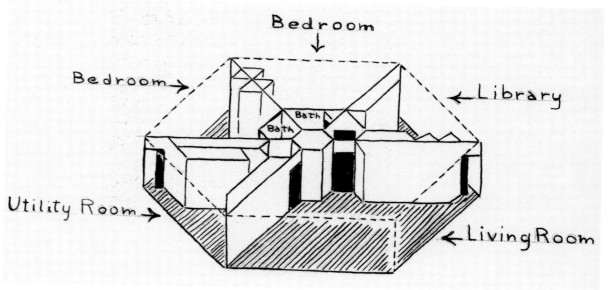

Divisions of living space in Dymaxion House, 1929

Artist's sketch of Dymaxion House with
Dymaxion Car, circa 1934

Variations on the 4D tower, circa 1928

Fuller's head sculpted by Isamu Noguchi,
1932

SHELTER

VOLUME 2   NUMBER 5

4. Shelter

SHELTER

STRUCTURAL STUDY ASSOCIATES SYMPOSIUM & 4 D ESSAYS

Cover of *Shelter*, no. 4, May 1932

A model, even a beautiful one, was not a finished product, and the 1930s were years in which Fuller tried to leverage the limited public attention that his Dymaxion House had brought to recruit support for transforming his seminal vision into an industry. The creation of a new industry, however, required financial resources that were very distant from the reach of R. Buckminster Fuller as he slept on the studio floors of sculptors Isamu Noguchi or Antonio Salemme, or the floor of a hotel where he was temporarily exhibiting the Dymaxion House model. After the real onset of the Depression, according to Fuller, he and his friend Noguchi "lived on coffee and doughnuts every other day or so"[26].

When asked by a potential investor for the cost of make a full-scale version of his Dymaxion House to be displayed at the 1933-4 Chicago World's Fair, Fuller retorted "100 million dollars", thus ending the conversation promptly. Fuller was referring to the cost of making the Dymaxion House a fully tooled industrial product ready for immediate production, rather than to making a hand-made mock-up, which offended his integrity. From a philosophical point of view, his point was valid. As Fuller argued, if for his new Model A Henry Ford had to make just one unit, that car would have cost $43,000,000 but the production of the second car would only cost an additional $500. Given that no housing industry existed, as yet, the cost of tooling all the mass-produced components for the new house would be substantially greater (and if anything, Fuller's estimate was conservative).

From a strategic point of view, however, this was a catastrophic mistake on Fuller's part. A full-size mock-up of the Dymaxion House and components at the Chicago World's Fair would arguably have brought Fuller's project major exposure, and the potential for serious industrial backing. Instead, Fuller's main promotional activities for his project in the 1930s were firstly through publication, passing from the mimeographic self-publication of *4D Timelock* to articles in *Fortune* and to his purchasing of the architectural magazine *T-Square*, which he rebaptized as *Shelter*, and secondly through developing sub-components of the larger project and a number of spin-off initiatives. He also developed a network of like-minded thinkers, though collaboration with Fuller was never on an entirely equal basis. Finally, he kept moving on the refinement of his Dymaxion House, culminating in the *Wichita Dymaxion Dwelling Machine* produced at Beech Aircraft plant in Kansas in 1944-46.

In spite of all his attempts at publicity, Fuller's 4D philosophy was only known to a handful of people in 1929. Moreover, as Bruce Barton had suggested, *4D Timelock*, even if it had been more widely accessible, was written in a dense "telegraphic" style that was unlikely to appeal to a broad public. The magazine *Architecture*, published by Charles Scribner and Sons, published a long editorial on Fuller's Dymaxion House in June 1929. Scribner also wanted to publish a book on Fuller's Dymaxion House. They

Cover of *Shelter*, no. 5, November 1932, depicting Isamu Noguchi's sculpture *Miss Expanding Universe*

The *Chronic Dis-Orders of Architecture*,
from *Shelter*, no. 4, May 1932

Comparing Dymaxion House to pig-pen
and other polygonal buildings, from *Shelter*,
no. 5, November 1932

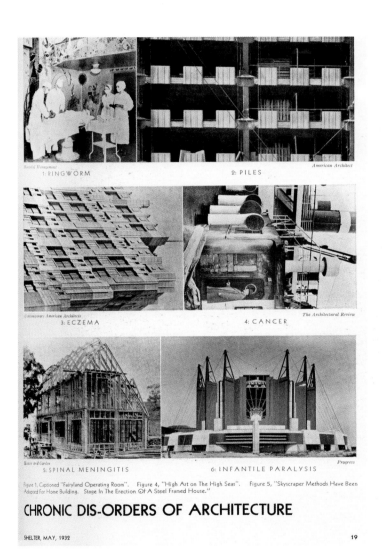

Figure 1, Captioned "Fairyland Operating Room". Figure 4, "High Art on The High Seas". Figure 5, "Skyscraper Methods Have Been Adapted For Home Building. Stage In The Erection Of A Steel Framed House."

CHRONIC DIS-ORDERS OF ARCHITECTURE

(1) Love Point Light, Eastern Shore, Maryland. (2) Goose Rock-light, North Haven, Maine. (3) Old Block house, Edgecombe, Maine. (4) Old Octagonal residence, Wiscasset, Maine. Designed as "Snugger" and to minimize wind whistle and settling distortion.

(5) Dymaxion House designed to withstand all forces which seek to penetrate or destroy human life process; and further to abet growth. (6) "Pig Incubator"—Economy Housing Corp., West Chicago, Ill., capacity 6 sows—sixty pigs—"saves your pigs in coldest weather" "farrows two litters per pig per year." Little pigs can huddle 'round heater in central ventilator—windows of cello-glass—allowing majority ultra-violet ray penetration—Price, $175.—Hogs have "money" value therefore have] had a scientific "break". "This little pig went to market,—."

STREAMLINED "UP"

Dr. Piccard's Stratosphere Transport, an unintentional advantage secured incidental to slack of balloon at starting level allowing for great expansion of gas in relatively low pressures of high altitudes. This streamline observation a teleological correlation.

Similar correlation observation found in similarity this picture to a carrot, also streamlined "up". Carrot moves slowly up through earth, held down as balloon by guy lines (roots) during growth period. Roots giving way at season's end so that with frost motion of ground carrot moves in direction least resistance, up to earth surface to rot and fertilize seed.

Since the last issue of Shelter a multitude of scientific attainments have been recorded of which this incident is but one.

Here are a few more that should eventually be correlated with Shelter service.

X-rays discovered capable of reversing as well as speeding up evolutionary processes. Cosmic radiation has energy of 40,000 million volts, 40 times previous estimates. Cosmic rays found stronger with increasing distance north and south of earth's equator. Certain types of diamond found photosensitive and productive of electric current. Effect differs from "electric eye" electron discharge. Visible light rays of longest wavelength will pass through nearly a foot of water with a loss of half their energy, whereas infrared radiations, with wavelengths only a little greater, have only one ten-thousandth as great a penetrating power. Most effective flesh-penetrating radiation found to be in very narrow band of wave lengths between dullest visible red and invisible infrared. Marconi bends short waves inbroadcasting. Heisenberg expounds new theory of neutron as "union" of electron and proton. Einstein estimates age of expanding universe, including earth, at 10 billion years.

Times Wide World

TELEOLOGY

PASS-AGE **7**

"WHAT DO YOU SEE?"—TELEOLOGICAL-DEMONSTRATION

Tension, gravity, timing, streaming, continuity, evolution, rhythm of relative identity, etc.—Typical specific correlation.—The dynamics of the hexagon (force diagram of circle) found in (A) "Centralization" as demonstrated in unification by circular-agglomeration (cable strands); in (B) "Decentralization" as demonstrated in expansion—by crystalization (snowflakes); in (C) "Abstraction" as demonstrated in elemental-synthesis (hydrocarbon-coronene). (Coronene recently developed, unknown in nature. Atomic structure: circle of 6 hexagons ("crown"), each consisting of 6 carbon atoms with 12 hydrogen atoms on circumference.) Pictures above:—(1 and 2) Olympic games events—girls diving, and sailing races. (4) Snowflakes, invariably six-sectored, never identical. (5 and 6) Scientific P. H. diffusing lights.

Drag around a streamlined 10 deck
Dymaxion Structure, 1932

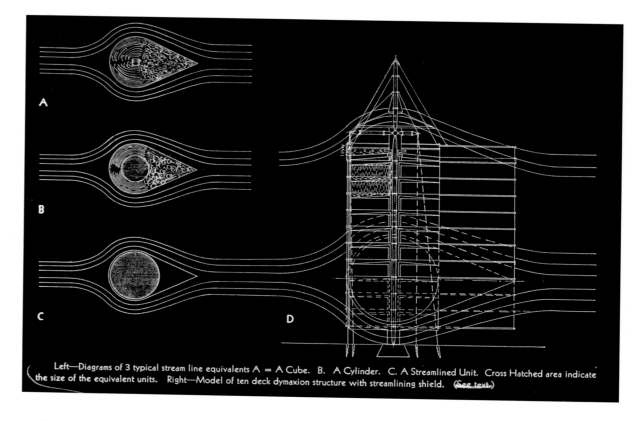

Left—Diagrams of 3 typical stream line equivalents A = A Cube. B. A Cylinder. C. A Streamlined Unit. Cross Hatched area indicate the size of the equivalent units. Right—Model of ten deck dymaxion structure with streamlining shield. (See text.)

made transcripts of Fuller's July 1929 lecture to members of the Architectural League in New York, with the view of writing them up in book form for interested laypersons, and even approached Lewis Mumford, later to be one of Fuller's most scathing critics, as a ghostwriter. The audience in this lecture included illustrious architects such as Raymond Hood, architect of the Chicago Tribune Tower, one of the only pieces of modern architecture that was singled out for praise in *4D Timelock*. Fuller noted that the building was "especially fine in many ways, but possibly its hexagonal rounding plan, bespeaking permanent individualism, is its most fundamental pleasantry, lacking the usual voluble hoggishness"[27]. After Fuller's lecture, the floor was opened to questioning that gives a unique picture of the dialogue between Fuller and the key architects of his day. Their questions were concerned with fleshing out the practical details of Fuller's design: "How do you get out of the elevator on the second floor?" was Hood's first question. Art Deco skyscraper architect Ralph T. Walker, quoted in the manuscript list of sources for *4D Timelock*, also participated in the lively discussion. In spite of Scribner's efforts, the book making Fuller's ideas available to a lay audience never appeared, perhaps as a consequence of the 1929 stock market crash.

In 1932, in search of an outlet for his philosophy, Fuller traded in his life insurance and purchased the architectural magazine *T-Square*. He renamed the magazine *Shelter*, and made it the official organ of a new loosely organized group called the Structural Studies Associates (SSA). *Shelter* proclaimed itself a "correlating medium for the forces of architecture". Contributors included Frank Lloyd Wright, Ely Jacques Kahn, Raymond Hood, Harvey Corbett, Richard Neutra and Philip Johnson. The SSA included Simon Breines and Knud Lönberg-Holm, who was very familiar with the Neues Bauen movement in Germany, and was also responsible for the clean design of the magazine. Everywhere, *Shelter* was permeated by Fuller's distinctive approach, from its editorial statements to its extraordinary photo essays. The overall philosophy of *Shelter* was "to do the most with the least", and it aimed to promote nothing less than the evolution of

"Buckminster Fuller, you are the most sensible man in New York, truly sensitive.
Nature gave you antennae, long-range finders you have learned to use."
Frank Lloyd Wright

Simon Breines, Dymaxion Gas Station, 1932

Model of Dymaxion Tower with streamlined fairing, 1932

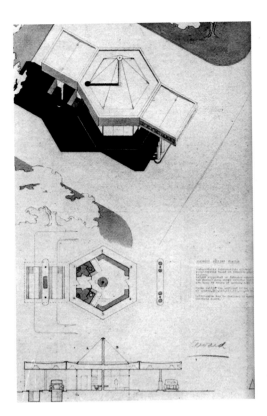

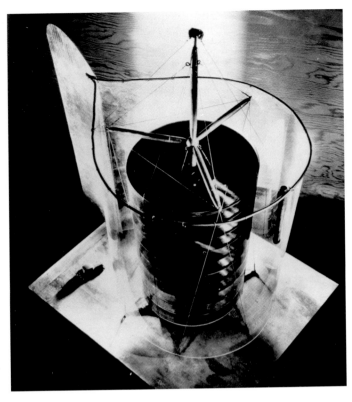

a "world-encompassing shelter industry". Fuller reorganized the magazine on naval principles – "officers of the deck" would take shifts in directing different issues. *Shelter* was meant to foster the economic, as opposed to iconoclastic dismissal of "traditional and compromise notions in architecture".

Fuller banned all advertising from *Shelter* – in a sense the whole magazine was advertising for his views, and he did not want to confuse the message. However, this move did not secure the long-term financial viability of the magazine, which only ran to three extraordinary issues. *Shelter* defined the problem of housing in the broadest possible terms, constantly pointing to improvements in aviation, shipping, and other areas of design that could be used to transform the home. The hexagonal Dymaxion House was compared to a hexagonal pigpen. In striking images, *Shelter* juxtaposed "habit bound inadequacy" – traditional housing destroyed by earthquakes, hurricanes and fires, with "force potential balance" – the simple equilibrium of tension and compression forces characteristic of good design, and "world-embracing force utilization" – the use of sound structural principles in building pylons and dirigible mooring masts. Wherever hide-bound tradition and "good taste" did not dictate style, Fuller found integrity of design principles, in "Revolvo display stands", lighthouses and pigpens, in snowflakes and rope-weaves.

In addition to promoting general design principles, *Shelter* allowed Fuller to launch new "spin-off" projects from the Dymaxion House, such as a noteworthy Dymaxion Gas Station designed by Simon Breines, and the Conning Tower, an ambitious multimedia center for executives with full projection facilities. In a sense, the Conning Tower, which took its name from the control center on warships, was a business version of the domestic "Go-ahead-with-Life" room, allowing a business owner to keep track of markets and competitors throughout the world.

Another ambitious tower project from this period was Fuller's *4D Tower Garage*, a double-spiral parking garage inscribed inside a conical shell, originally designed for the Chicago World's Fair of 1933.

Early drawing of 4D Transport with
inflatable wings and a double-tetrahedral
frame, 1928

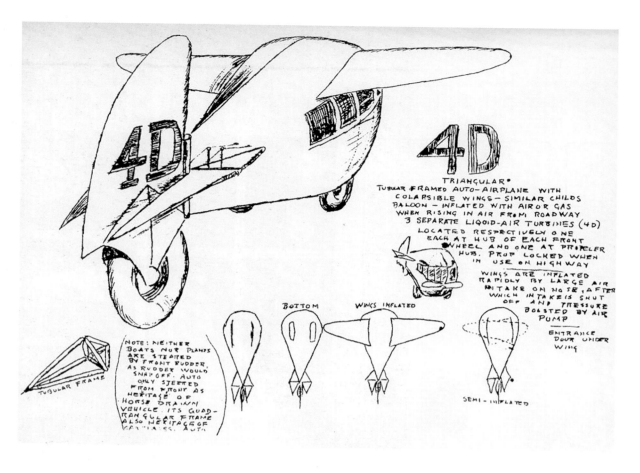

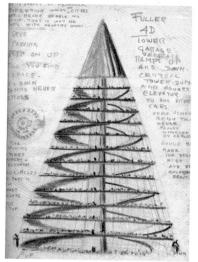

4D Tower Garage, proposal for 1933
Chicago World's Fair

Fuller's annotation reads "Fuller 4D Tower Garage, separate ramps up and down: central tower supports and houses elevator to and from cars.... could be made 100 decks high and be colossally beautiful". Fuller also remarked "this is a sample of mechanical perfection that old cities would never be able to permit. That is why 4D starts with country work", i.e. rural architecture gave more freedom for innovation, given the complex building codes stifling innovation in the urban environment.

The final, November 5 1932 issue of *Shelter* bore on its cover a sculpture by Noguchi, a streamlined aluminium-cast portrait of Chicago choreographer and dancer Ruth Page, renamed by Fuller *Miss Expanding Universe*. This issue marked the entry of a new theme into Fuller's oeuvre, the theme of streamlining and the contrary concept of "drag". The issue also contained a programmatic essay by Fuller on streamlining. Typically, Fuller was to reject the "cosmetic streamlining" becoming popular among automobile and train designers of the 1930s, in favour of serious experimentation in wind tunnels. This issue contained photographs of a ten-storey *Streamlined Dymaxion Shelter*, a reworking of the *4D Lightful Towers* suspended from a central mast. Fuller claimed that placing streamlined shields around a square skyscraper would reduce its drag by wind-stress by at least 87 percent. In turn, this would reduce the heat-loss from the building by at least 87 percent. A large fin or rudder attached to the shield caused the whole thing to rotate depending on prevailing wind-direction, ensuring that the building always presented its most streamlined profile to the wind.

Wind-tunnel experimentation also guided the development of another important project, namely the *Dymaxion Transport*. Fuller's 1928 mimeographed drawings had featured one drawing of the *4D Transport*, a "triangular tubular framed auto-airplane". This vehicle was designed to have inflatable wings and

Isamu Noguchi's gypsum wind-tunnel
model of the 4D Transport, 1932

Sketch of the 4D Transport from *Shelter*,
no. 5, November 1932

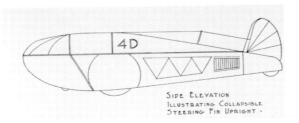

SIDE ELEVATION
ILLUSTRATING COLLAPSIBLE
STEERING FIN UPRIGHT.

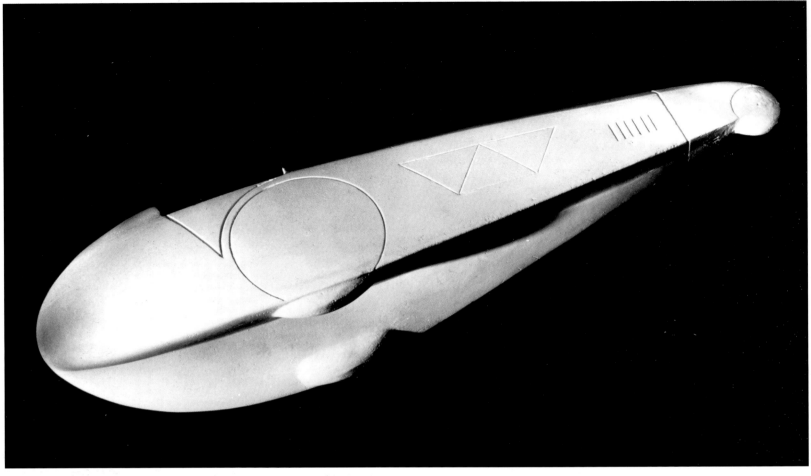

Isamu Noguchi's gypsum wind-tunnel
model of the 4D Transport, 1932

500,000 BC – 1850

1850 – 1950

1950 – – –

man on earth

Man on Earth – the transition from isolated
communities to seafarers and air-transport,
three illustrations for Fuller's preface to
Ladislav Sutnar, *Transport*, brochure, 1950

Airflow around a flat plate, a Ford sedan and an ideal streamline form, *Shelter*, no. 5, November 1932

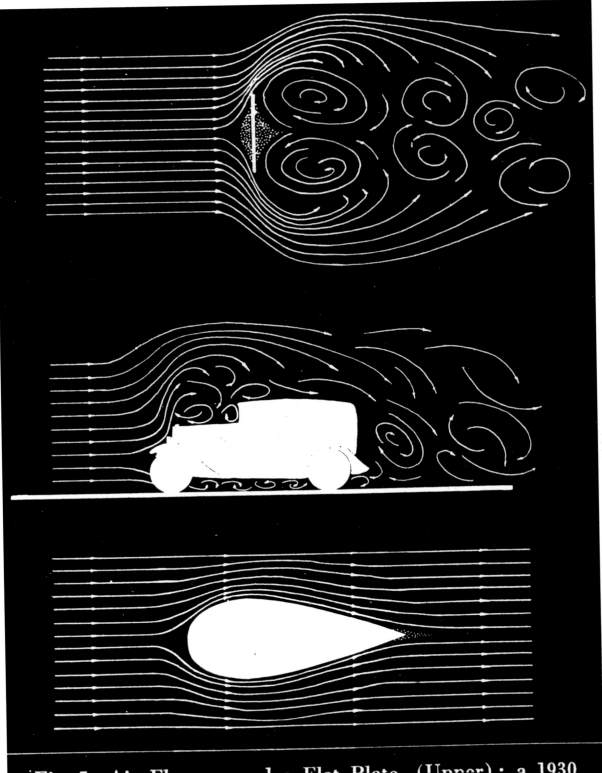

Fig. 7—Air Flow around a Flat Plate, (Upper); a 1930 Sedan (Middle); and an Ideal Streamline Form (Lower)

a propeller, which would be locked when in use on the highway. The tubular frame of Fuller's earliest design is made up of a pair of tetrahedra, one elongated to a point, an early example of Fuller's use of the tetrahedron in design. Fuller's Dymaxion Transport, which also featured in his second Dymaxion House model, was intended to be steered from the back. Fuller remarked tersely that "Neither boats nor planes are steered by front rudder, as rudder would snap off. Auto only steered from front as heritage of horse-drawn vehicle. Its quadrangular frame also heritage of carriages". Fuller later suggested the use of "jet-stilts" to allow the vehicle to take off vertically. To his daughter Allegra, he described the three-wheeled vehicle as a "zoomobile", explaining that it could hop off the road at will, fly about, then, as deftly as a bird, settle back into a place in traffic.

"I knew people would call it an automobile, but it wasn't designed to be just an automobile. It was designed, as I said, to become an omnimedium, wing-less, flying device with angularly orientable twin jet-stilts – like the jets coming out from beneath the wings of a duck."

Given Fuller's vision of air-delivered housing, a personal auto-airplane seems like a necessary development, otherwise, the occupants of a Dymaxion House would be dependent on a pre-existing transport infrastructure. In the case of the automobile, additionally, an industry already existed, so the development of a true prototype of Fuller's 4D Transport was not inconceivable, even with limited capital investment. As Fuller put it, "the reason I built an advanced design car rather than an advanced design house was simply because I knew I could draw on the already available inventory of parts from the automotive world. There was nothing like that available for housing".

Isamu Noguchi made gypsum models of the 4D Transport on the basis of Fuller's early designs, for wind tunnel testing. In the November 1932 issue of *Shelter*, the initial designs for the 4D Transport were published for the first time. It was compared to a fish or a zeppelin, designed to reduce drag. Fuller remarked in his essay on *Streamlining* in the same issue that "Planes and ships are steered from behind; if they had a rudder in front it would break off"[28].

In January 1933, Fuller was given $5,000 by stockbroker Philip Pearson, and was able to commence work on building the 4D Transport, at least for "extended ground-taxiing". The following month he rented the Dynamometer building of the defunct Locomobile Company's factory in Bridgeport, Connecticut. He engaged a crew of six world-class craftsmen out of a thousand applicants to work on the project under the direction of seaplane and racing yacht designer Starling Burgess, who was extremely influential on the final design. Burgess, who first called on Fuller in the Winthrop hotel on October 9 1932, had worked on the streamlined fairing for the Dymaxion Shelter, and the central mast of the Dymaxion House. The final design of the Dymaxion Car, with its wooden-ribs and nautical interior, owed much to Burgess's experience with racing yacht design.

An experimental chassis was completed six-weeks after work had begun, but the single rear wheel developed oscillations at speed. To complete the car in time for the 1933 Chicago World's Fair, the crew was expanded to 28. By July, the first complete car, incorporating a standard 85 horsepower Ford V8 engine, donated by Henry Ford himself at 70% discount, was finished, and bore the new "Dymaxion" logo depicting a flying fish. Driving through Manhattan, the car caused a sensation, and gridlock. Excluded from the automobile show at Madison Square Garden, Fuller parked it near the entrance, causing further traffic jams. The car could reportedly reach speeds of up to 120 mph. Rear wheel steering, which used cables and pulleys very similar to those used in aircraft, proved problematic, causing the car to "drift", especially in the presence of cross-winds.

In October 1933, the first Dymaxion Car arrived in Chicago for the Century of Progress Worlds'

024 - 7/13/33 Buckminster Full__ Body Mc

Working on the Dymaxion Car in
Bridgeport, Connecticut, 1933

Skeleton of the Dymaxion Car, 1933

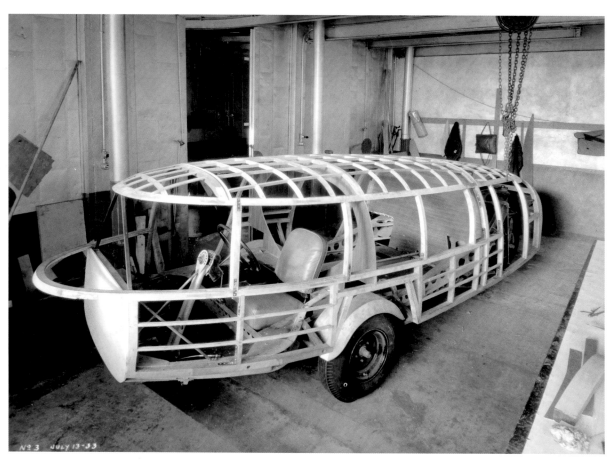

The Dymaxion Car alongside a
contemporary Ford, 1933

The Dymaxion Car in front of the Crystal
House at the Chicago World's Fair, 1934
Courtesy the Estate of R Buckminster
Fuller, Sebastopol, CA, and Courtesy of
Department of Special Collections, Stanford
University Libraries, Stanford, CA

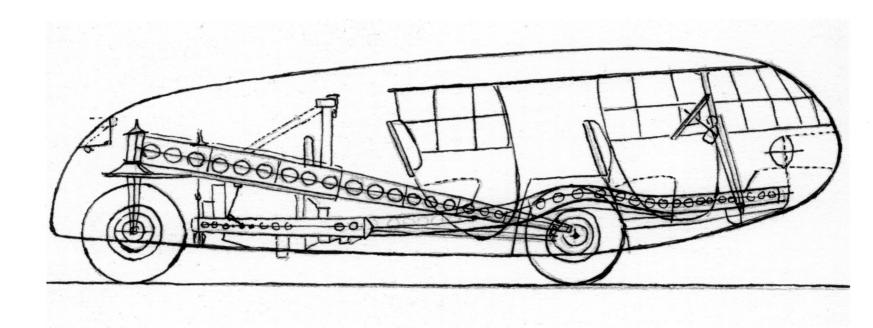

Fair. In addition to the Dymaxion Car, the Chicago Fair boasted a great number of attractions, contrasting "quaint", primitive theme villages, such as the "Midget Village" and "Merrie England" with futuristic experiences like the "Skyride" in which rocket cars whisked passengers between two 628-foot towers. Streamlined design dominated the production automobiles on exhibition, which included a gold-plated Packard, and the Lincoln Zephyr. On October 26, 1933 Commander Hugo Eckener brought the Graf Zeppelin to the Chicago Fair.

Two of the Zeppelin's passengers were taken for a ride in the Dymaxion Car. Unfortunately, there was a major crash just outside the Fair grounds, when another car bumped the tail of the Dymaxion, killing one of the passengers and seriously injuring another. Not knowing about the second car, the newspapers assumed that the unusual design of the car must have been responsible for the crash, with headlines such as "Freak Auto Turns Over With Graf Passengers" and some potential investors were scared off. A second car was produced, and finally a third, made for conductor Leopold Stokowski, which had a rear-view periscope and a central fin to stop the car from wobbling. The third car was exhibited outside William Keck's Crystal House in the Chicago Worlds' Fair. Keck had built a House of Tomorrow for the 1933 Fair that was twelve sided and had an airplane hangar instead of a garage, containing a replica of Lindbergh's *Spirit of St. Louis* and a Pierce-Arrow Silver Arrow, almost a direct quotation of Fuller's Dymaxion House. Keck's *House of Tomorrow* indicates Fuller's enormous missed opportunity to exhibit a mock-up of the Dymaxion House at the Fair. The design of the Crystal House was strongly influenced, if not actually created, by Lee Atwood in Keck's office, who had also collaborated on the ill-fated patent drawings for Fuller's 4D House, adding insult to injury.

In 1934 the third Dymaxion Car was admired by both H.G. Wells, who used a similar vehicle in the film version of *Things to Come* and Christopher Morley, who composed a poem about the car, *STREAM-LINES (Thoughts in a Dymaxion Car)*.

"I'm interested in this not just as a car, which is relatively unimportant,

But as a symbol of what is forward in every phase of living.

Dymaxion Car blueprint, 1934

Not only in locomotion, architecture, shipbuilding, but in morals and manners, clothes, religions, even in literature

We grope for the Streamline: to reduce unnecessary wind resistance"[29]

However, the bad publicity caused by the crash of the first car, the abysmal investment climate and financial mismanagement, not to mention a falling-out between Burgess and Fuller, mitigated against the Dymaxion Car ever going into mass production. The first car was repaired and used by the owners, Gulf Oil, in a publicity campaign. The second car (which is the only surviving one, now in the National Automobile Museum in Reno, Nevada) was eventually donated to the mechanics who made it, to compensate for back-wages, and the third car disappeared, being reportedly cut up for scrap during the Korean war.

Another pressing task for Fuller in bringing his 4D vision into being was the development of a bathroom for his Dymaxion House. As he remarked in 1968, "modern architecture is just so many nozzles on the invisible sewer system"[30], and if one wanted to industrialize the home it made a good deal of sense to start with the bathroom. The *Dymaxion Bathroom* was developed between 1930 and 1938 and is the component of his vision for industrially produced housing that came closest to true mass-production. The first prototype was designed in 1930 for American Standard Sanitary Heating and Plumbing Company. The final, patented design was produced for Phelps Dodge Copper Company. The whole bathroom was conceived as a unit made up of four pieces that were clamped together to make the complete bathroom. The pieces were pre-plumbed and wired. Fuller envisaged this being installed in small homes, and even allowing renters to bring their bathrooms with them when they moved home. The seamless, die-stamped metal components rendered the bathroom hygienic and easy to clean. A fan, under the sink, sucked down to remove steam and unpleasant odours. The mirror was mounted on the inside of the medicine-cabinet door, to keep it free from condensation. The sink's nozzle was located in the side towards the user, directing the flow of water away, to avoid splashing clothes. The components of the bathroom were light enough to be carried by two men and could be installed in a home and ready to use in three hours.

Later, Fuller anticipated replacing the bathtub altogether with a fog-gun shower, which would

Dymaxion logo, circa 1934

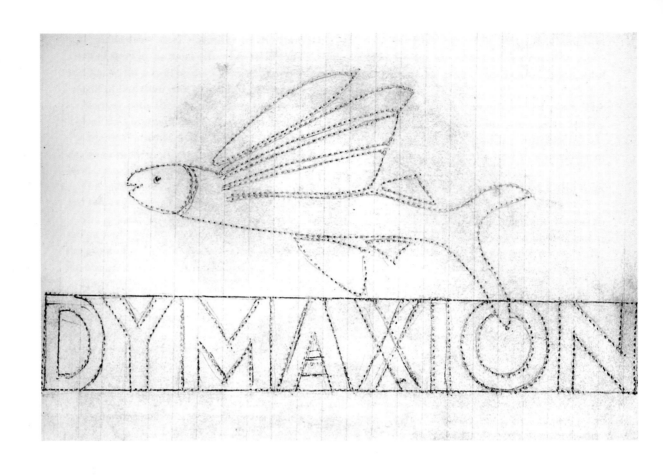

H.G. Wells with the Dymaxion Car, 1934

TEN CENTS A COPY

The Saturday Review

of LITERATURE

EDITED BY HENRY SEIDEL CANBY

VOLUME X   NEW YORK, SATURDAY, JUNE 2, 1934   NUMBER 46

Exiles from Reality

BY BERNARD DE VOTO

MR. MALCOLM COWLEY has undertaken to write the history of the lost generation.* He identifies this generation as the group of writers who saw service in the Army, lived in Greenwich Village for a while, expatriated themselves on behalf of the good life, and finally returned to make what terms they could with the America from which they had seceded. It is not clear just how or wherein these people were lost, nor just why an explanation of them is desirable, but "Exile's Return" is an effort to tell their story in relation to the infinite.

Mr. Cowley's book will be an easy exercise for Freudians. Much the most important fact about the generation, the author tells us, was the process of deracination to which it was subjected and from whose effects only a part of it recovered. The mandrake has an important place in art and folklore: uprooting is a symbol of emasculation. The sense of personal enfeeblement, of power and identity lost, is usually associated with the castration complex. When a fixation occurs

than Mr. Cowley assumes. The importance of literary people is chiefly to one another; a fixed difference between the voice of a nation and the manifesto of a house organ must be taken into account.

The literary first, since it was probably the literary whom Miss Gertrude Stein meant when she uttered a phrase that must eventually lose its tragic connotation. There are a good many writers who were of draft-age or below it in 1917 but who nevertheless failed to suffer the uprooting, the frustration, and the despair that Mr. Cowley describes with such eloquence. What, in terms of Mr. Cowley's book, is to be made of them? One may say that they are unimportant writers; one may assert that they have no relation to the true spirit of the times or the genuine current of social and intellectual and emotional movement, or that they are counter-revolutionary phenomena. But such a judgment is flagrantly subjective—it is to define importance of the true and the genuine as what I hold to be important and true and genuine, and that is not at all the burden of Mr. Cowley's book. There they

THE SHAPE OF THINGS TO COME CONFRONTS MR. WELLS
The author, during his recent visit to America, with the new Dymaxion car, photographed for The Saturday Review by Robert Disraeli.

Wells the Fantasiast

SEVEN FAMOUS NOVELS. By H. G. Wells. The Time Machine; The Island

in a good gripping dream. . . . The living interest lies in their non-fantastic elements and not in the invention itself. . . . The thing that makes such imaginations interesting is their translation

spray atomized water to clean the body. Fuller, who had noticed the ability of fog to remove engine-grease from his face while in the Navy was keen to conserve water wherever possible, with a view to autonomy, and claimed that a satisfying shower was possible using just one pint of water. Another unusual planned feature of the Dymaxion Bathroom that was never fully developed was a waterless Packaging Toilet, designed to pack human waste to be used in fertilizers and the chemical industry. Fuller's lifelong thought-experiment of fully autonomous living encouraged him to deal with the practicalities of recycling and sustainable design long before the environmentalist movement had popularized these notions. For Fuller, these concerns were entirely practical.[31]

But what of the development of the house design itself during this period? In 1932 Fuller worked with other Structural Studies Associates on a design for a twenty person dormitory for migrant farm workers and factory workers in Russia. The design, which dates from around 1932, was similar to the Dymaxion House – a tension structure hanging from a central mast on a hexagonal base. Most of the structure was made of wood and locally available materials. Wall panels could open like petals, and their aluminium-coated surfaces reflected sunlight and the heat of the kerosene burner. A rudder on the roof vent controlled drag and ventilation. The building was designed to be towed to a site by a tractor, and erected by the future occupants in an hour.[32] The tractor would also provide compressed air and serve as a generator for the shelter. The 1930s industrialization of the U.S.S.R. was of enormous interest to the SSA. The need to rehouse agricultural and factory workers on a massive scale presented a potential blank canvas for innovative design while the U.S. was struggling under the Depression, and hindered by zoning and building regulations. This theme occupied much of the final November 1932 issue of *Shelter*. The tractor-powered *Dymaxion Mobile Dormitories* never went into production for reasons that remain obscure.

The onset of World War II brought new demand for light, emergency shelters for displaced families. In anticipation of the bombing of British cities, the British War Relief Organization invited Fuller to design such a shelter in 1940. While driving through the Midwest with his friend writer Christopher Morley, Fuller noticed the mass-produced steel grain-bins made by the Butler company, and realized that the transformation of such a bin into a livable house would not require vast expenditure.

The final product, while it dispensed with Fuller's characteristic central mast, relying instead on the support of its outer shell, was built with the aid of a hoist. Fuller realized, while building the prototype, that when the *Dymaxion Deployment Unit* was held above the ground by the hoist, the hot air inside the house went downward and out under the skirt of the structure, with cool air coming in at the top, contrary to his expectations, causing the interior of the unit to remain cool in the hot Kansas sun. This natural "chilling effect" was a subject of fascination to Fuller, as an illustration of the building's potential to work as a climate control. Although the British government backed away from the project (their steel was needed to make armaments) the Dymaxion Deployment Unit was used by Russian and American mechanics and airmen in World War II, especially in the Persian Gulf. While it never went into true mass-production, a number of units were actually produced and used. As a cylindrical structure topped with a conoidal roof, the DDU also worked well as a modular unit – doors could be installed anywhere to connect two units. One of the more interesting modules was a four-foot diameter cylindrical bathroom unit, with a septic tank in the cylinder's base and a water-tank above the ceiling.

Like many of Fuller's projects, military adoption of the DDU proved far easier than civilian use

Patent drawing for Dymaxion Bathroom, 1940

Dymaxion Bathroom, undated

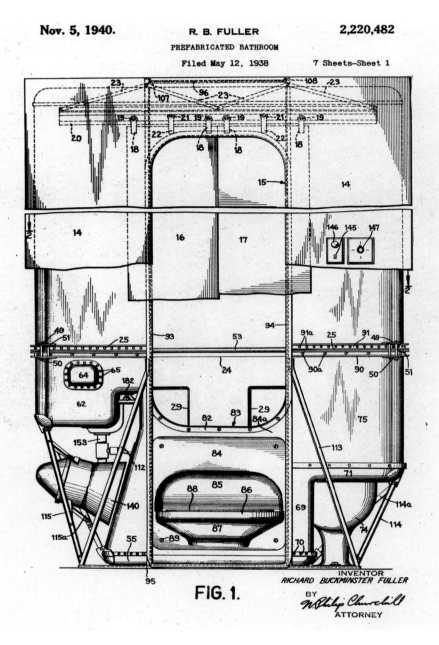

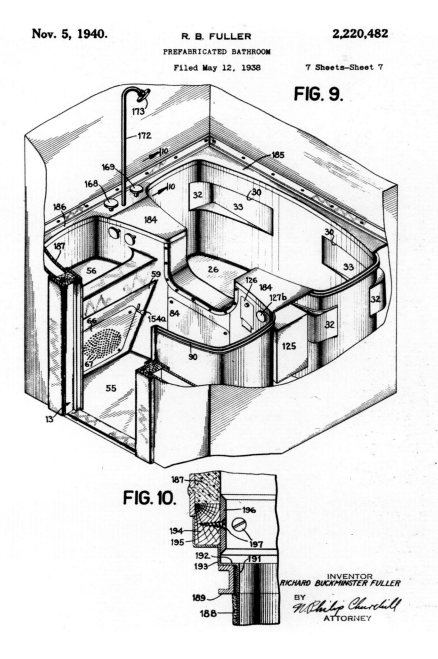

Nov. 5, 1940.   R. B. FULLER   2,220,482

PREFABRICATED BATHROOM

Filed May 12, 1938   7 Sheets—Sheet 7

FIG. 9.

FIG. 10.

INVENTOR
RICHARD BUCKMINSTER FULLER

BY
N. Philip Churchill
ATTORNEY

Structural Associates sketches for
Dymaxion 20-worker shelter, for Russian
Cooperative farming, 1931-2

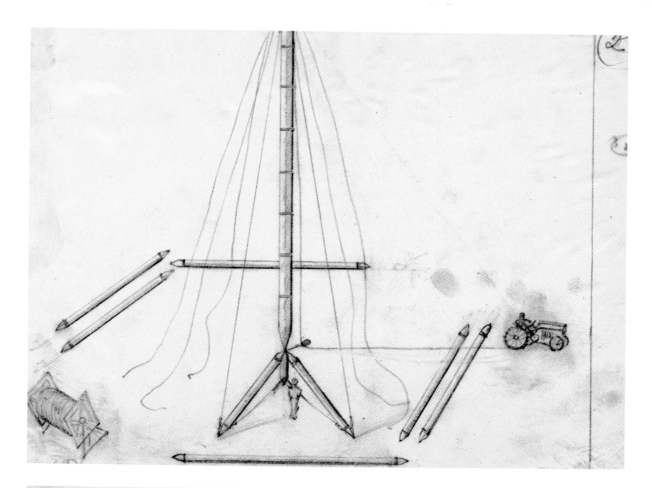

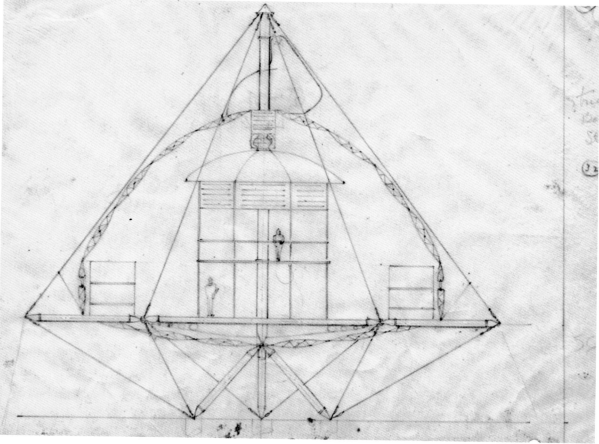

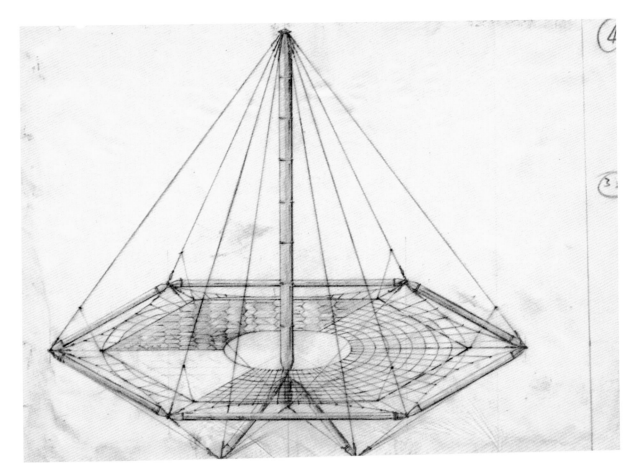

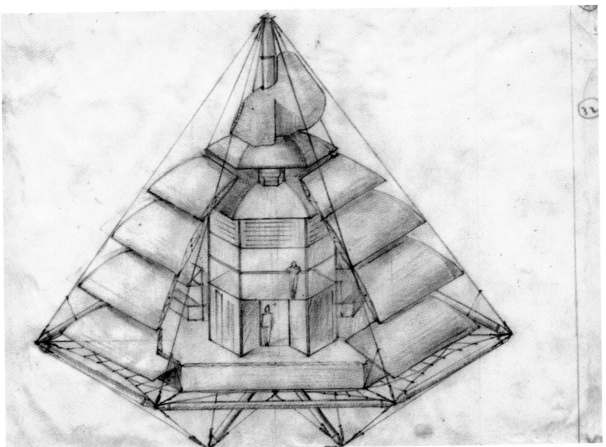

– selling a project to military commanders was a very different matter from marketing to the working-class family. For Fuller, since his experience in the Navy, the military remained a site for experimentation with new materials, technologies and principles which would only slowly trickle down for the benefit of the civilian population.

Fuller's 1944-46 Dymaxion Dwelling Machine, or the *Wichita House* was a direct example of trying to convert weaponry into what Fuller called "livingry". "Livingry" meant the use of the latest technical innovations not for military purposes, as was generally the case, but to enhance the lives of people throughout the world and release them from drudgery and vulnerability to fire, famine and disease. As Fuller later put it in the introduction to his 1981 book *Critical Path*: "With the highest aeronautical and engineering facilities of the world redirected from weaponry to livingry production, all humanity would have the option of becoming enduringly successful"[33].

The Beech Aircraft plant in Wichita, Kansas, was the main center of bomber production during World War II. The Midwest location was chosen to reduce the risk of missile attack on the base. With the end of the war rapidly approaching, in 1944, many employees of the aircraft plant were leaving the base, due to fears of a decline in demand and bad housing conditions. Fuller had presented the military with drawings of a modified aluminium house, built around a central mast and raised off the ground. This "Air-barac" Dymaxion Dwelling Machine could be arranged as officer housing, barracks, and even as a multi-storey hospital. In 1944, Beech Aircraft decided to use their state-of-the-art facility and highly trained aircraft engineers to realize Fuller's Dymaxion Dwelling Machine. The project helped stem the exodus of workers due to the slacking off of the demand for bombers.

Between 1944 and 1946, work was carried out to make two prototypes. Like the Russian 20-person worker dormitories, the Dymaxion Dwelling Machine (DDM) had a rotating vent at the top fitted with a rudder. The most sophisticated aircraft technology available was being applied to housing. The DDM was designed to resist the tornadoes that were frequent in Kansas. The completed structure weighed about 3 tons and could be shipped in a cylindrical container designed to fit in an aircraft cargo compartment. When assembled, the central mast of the Dymaxion Dwelling Machine looked like a cross between an umbrella and the hub of a bicycle wheel.

The first prototype was erected indoors. There was a disagreement about the kind of furniture that would be appropriate. Fuller wanted pneumatic and tension furniture, similar to the furniture that had adorned the 1929 Dymaxion House. However, the Beech Aircraft officials insisted that the interior should look familiar to prospective buyers, to compensate for the circular aluminium exterior, so they filled it with normal middle-class furniture – heavy armchairs and beds, chests of drawers, and even a grand piano. One can imagine Fuller's reactions. There were also some design innovations in the furnishings though: the Dymaxion Dwelling Machine came with a Dymaxion Bathroom, and was also equipped with the O-volving shelves that Fuller had imagined for the 1928-9 Dymaxion House. These were shelves made to rotate at the flick of a switch. The media coverage of the Dymaxion Dwelling Machine produced significant public interest. Around 3,500 orders came in (not the 30,000 that Fuller would sometimes claim).

Fuller seems to have strongly resisted the attempts by the Beech Aircraft Corporation to bring the Dymaxion Dwelling Machine to market, in part due to a desire to perfect the design. Additionally, the project ran into obstacles with union codes and financial difficulties caused by the large retooling costs for

Dymaxion Deployment Units, 1940

Butler grain-bin, used as basis for Dymaxion
Deployment Unit, 1930

Modular combination of Dymaxion
Deployment Units with plan, 1940

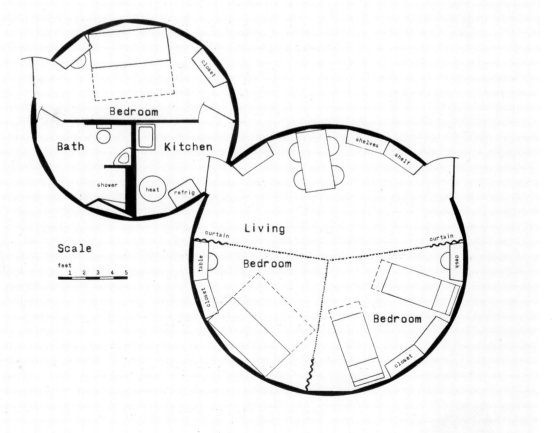

Interior of Butler Dymaxion Deployment
Unit, 1940

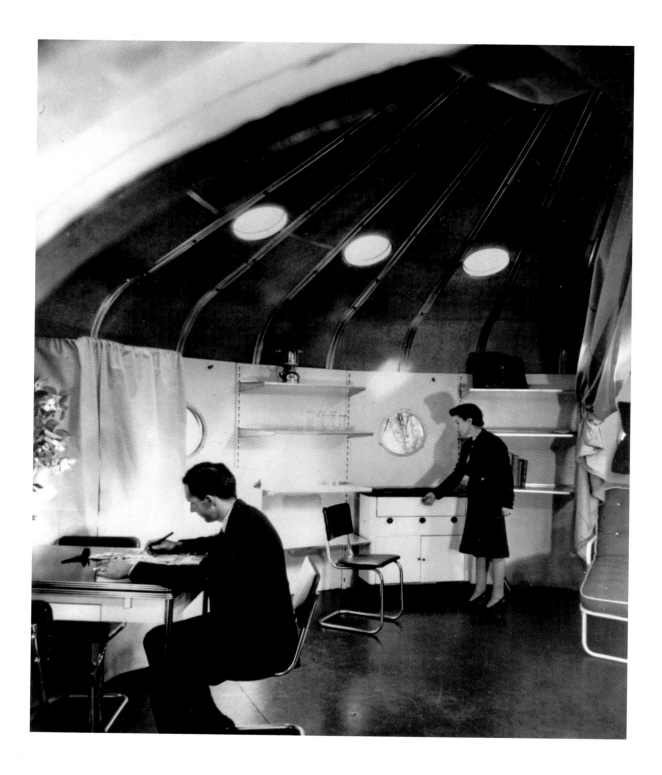

Interior of Butler Dymaxion Deployment
Unit, 1940

Advertising shot of interior of Dymaxion
Deployment Unit, 1940

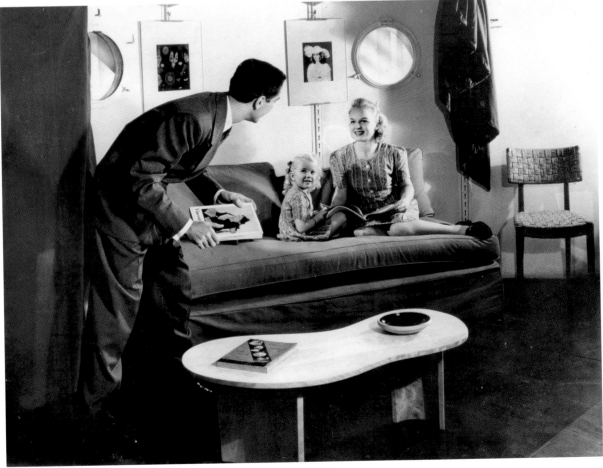

Mock-up of a Dymaxion Dwelling Machines
village, undated

Dymaxion Dwelling Unit, artist's
impression, undated

Sectional view of Dymaxion Dwelling
Machine, 1946

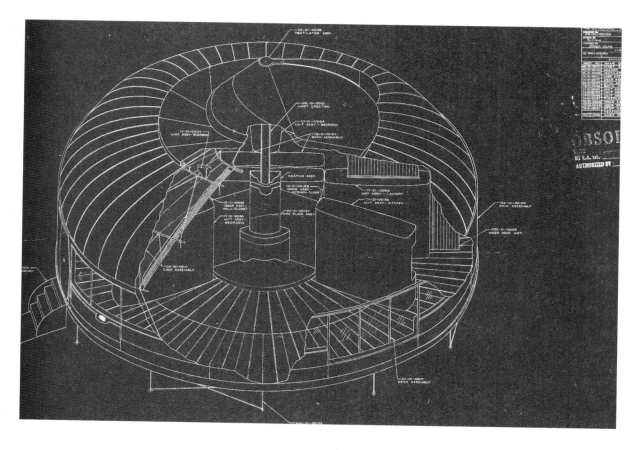

true mass-production. There were features of the house that were only half completed: the rotating air-vent at the top of the house tended to suck out air, as the rudder automatically moved the opening down-wind of the house. However, the "chilling" convection currents that Fuller had observed in the 1940 Dymaxion Deployment Unit had the opposite effect, namely to suck air in at the top and expel it through air-vents at the skirting.

Finally, the *Wichita House* – the one completed model of the Dymaxion Dwelling Machine – was sold for one dollar to a local business man named Graham, who rebuilt it on his land, and made several "additions" using conventional materials, to Fuller's dismay. His six children lived in it and "played" on the structure as a giant musical instrument, exploiting a feature of Fuller's tension-based buildings. A great advantage of the use of aluminum was the lack of need for maintenance. However steel rivets were used in the version that was built, creating small electrolytic currents in the presence of the water that leaked through the roof and leading to galvanic corrosion. After the Wichita House was vacated by the Graham family, due to a disputed inheritance, it appears to have become, for a short time, a house of ill-repute, and was even painted pink to entice the airmen as they flew into Wichita! Subsequently, the house was abandoned and invaded by raccoons until the 1990s when it was removed and restored to its former glory in the Ford Museum at Dearborn, Michigan.

How did the Wichita House of 1946 differ from Fuller's 1928-9 vision for the Dymaxion House? In a fundamental sense, Fuller's 1928-9 vision implied embracing a radically new lifestyle, and philosophy of physical, intellectual and social autonomy. In some ways, the Wichita House was a toned-down version of the original vision, a compromise that evolved through long negotiations with designers, mechanics, the Board of Directors of Beech Aircraft and other parties. In another sense, while less radical, the Wichita House

Study of convection currents in Dymaxion
Dwelling Machine

Model of Dymaxion Dwelling Machine with
furnishings, 1946

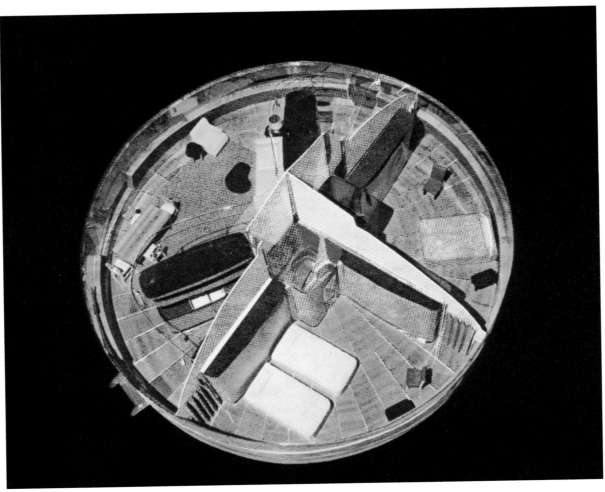

was a design improvement on the original Dymaxion House. Between 1928 and 1946, Fuller had discovered wind, and considered streamlining, drag and convection currents as factors to be considered in housing design. In the path towards the Dymaxion Dwelling Machine or Wichita House, he analyzed buildings as "little ships whose standard cruising speed is 12 miles an hour, but which suddenly are accelerated to 30 miles an hour, and then suddenly again have to go 50 miles an hour, and sometimes they have to go 70 miles an hour, and then the flat planking begins to fly off as flat boards develop lift in parallel with the wind, which lift is opposed only by the friction of the nails amounting to but a few pounds in tension as nail-pulling experience confirms"[34].

Considering buildings as "little ships" provided with rudders that rotated with the wind was a new direction in housing design. Fuller was not merely concerned with heat-loss through drag, but also with the dangers posed to buildings by high winds. In 1964, a tornado passed within 300 yards of the Wichita House, without inflicting any damage on the structure, suggesting that, even if the house never went into mass-production and was yet another business failure, Fuller's experiment with wind was a remarkable success.

Convection currents inside Wichita House, 1946

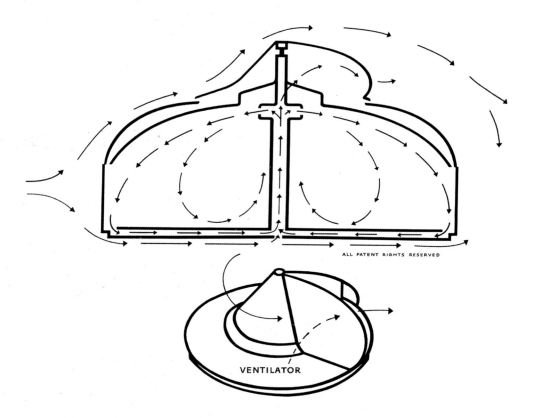

ALL PATENT RIGHTS RESERVED

VENTILATOR

[26] Robert Snyder, *An Autobiographical Monologue/Scenario*, St. Martin's Press, New York, p. 58.
[27] Fuller, *4D Timelock*, cit.
[28] Fuller, "Streamlining", in *Shelter*, no. 5, November 1932.

[29] Christopher Morley, *STREAMLINES (Thoughts in a Dymaxion Car)*, excerpt, *The Saturday Review*, March 31, 1934.
[30] *The Listener*, 26 September 1968, transcribed by John Donat.
[31] Jay Baldwin, *Bucky Works: Buckminster Fuller's*

Ideas for Today, Wiley, New York, 1996, pp.30-34.
[32] Baldwin, *Bucky Works*, cit., pp. 36-28.
[33] R. Buckminster Fuller, *Critical Path*, St. Martins Press, 1981, p. xxv.
[34] *Designing a New Industry* (1946), 31 ff, quoted in YPS, pp. 238-9.

Wichita House wind-test model, 1946

Wichita House model, 1946

O-volving shelves, circa 1946

Wichita House, on completion of
installation, 1946

Interior of Wichita House, 1946

The Dymaxion Dwelling Machine, interior,
1946

Fuller's profile of the Industrial Revolution, 1943

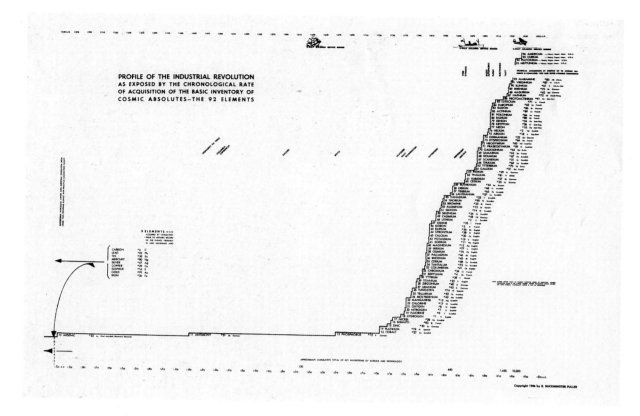

Chart of world industrialization, 1952

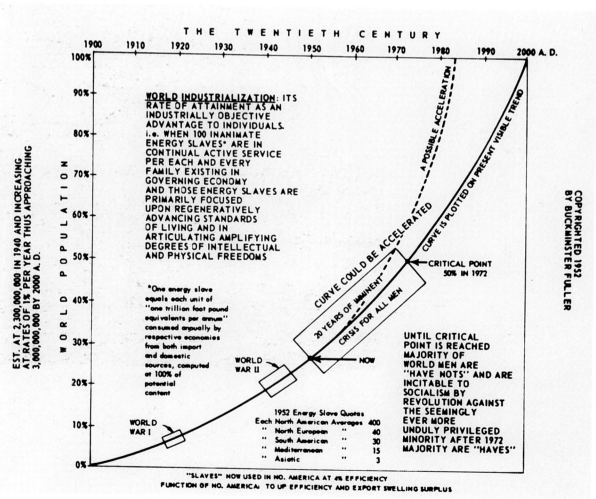

Mechanical Wing, a trailer containing "the mechanical essentials of contemporary U.S. living", reprinted from *The Architectural Forum*, October 1940.

Born 1895, Milton, Mass. Inventor machines, building products, Dymaxion house, Dymaxion car, one-piece prefabricated bathroom. Outstanding exponent of industrialization of building. Author "Nine Chains to the Moon." At present technical consultant to "Fortune."

THE MECHANICAL WING is a

compact, mobile package in which the mechanical essentials of contemporary U. S. living can be transported to the Vermont farmhouse, lakeside camp site, week-end or vacation house, or incorporated in a permanent dwelling.

It is attached to a tubular steel A-frame trailer, frame integral with axle. Attaches to car by ball joint hitch, weight sprung by car. Has integral jacks on casters for maneuvering by hand, blocking up Wing, etc. A-frame alone is useful as luggage, fuel, boat and water carrier, also as a crane for manipulating heavy objects. Note hinged-up tubular barrel chock.

Bath-dressing room unit supplied optionally with (1) water line connection where running water available, (2) combination compressed-air, water

and chemical fog-gun cleansing devices, (3) hermetically sealed waste packaging and chemical disposal apparatus.

The energy unit is located between bath and kitchen. Contains diesel engine (h.p. optional), electrical generator, air compressor and tank, battery and radiator. The last uses domestic hot water to warm incoming air. The fan shown can be reversed in summer to exhaust warm air from living units.

Kitchen and laundry unit, with sink, laundry tub, electric range and refrigerator, storage space for dishes, silver and linen. Dry warm storage shelves over diesel above sink.

Side walls: waterproof, synthetic-resin-glued plywood truss. Walls and floors of the three units

(Continued on page 92)

Reprinted from THE ARCHITECTURAL FORUM, October, 1940

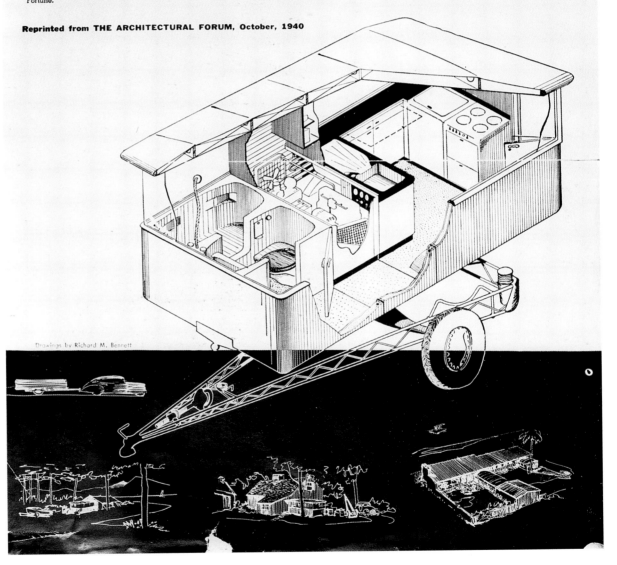

Drawings by Richard M. Bennett

5. Early geodesic experiments

One World Island Map from *Nine Chains to the Moon*, 1938

Fuller's structures up to and including the 1946 Wichita House were basically horizontal planes, hung from a vertical central axis. A partial exception was the Butler Dymaxion Deployment Unit (DDU), which did not have a central mast, given its evolution from a pre-existing steel grain bin. However, installation of the DDU made essential use of central suspension. More importantly, the symmetry of the DDU related to one privileged axis, the vertical axis. While Fuller had challenged the predominance of rectangular structures in the horizontal plane, experimenting with hexagonal and circular floor-plans, his structures still made concessions to perpendicularity in being organized around a single vertical axis. In the early 1940s, Fuller embarked on a path of experimentation that was to lead him to design structures with multiple, non-orthogonal axes of symmetry that apparently defied gravity. His point of departure was nothing less than the world itself.

In 1935, while compiling statistical analyses concerning world copper usage for the Phelps Dodge Corporation, Fuller began to be dissatisfied with the most popular means for representing the world on a flat sheet, the Mercator projection, which grossly distorted distances close to the poles, by representing lines of longitude as parallel lines. Fuller was especially interested in trying to represent the relative sizes of land-masses correctly for the purposes of data analysis (in the standard Mercator projection, Greenland appears to be close to the size of Africa, whereas in reality it is about one thirteenth the size of Africa). Fuller, who had been interested in representations of the globe since his 4D sketches of 1928, experimented with a world map that had the North Pole at its centre. While not yet formulated into a rigorous cartographic technique, this point of view had the advantage of making the whole world appear to be a single landmass surrounded by a single ocean, what Fuller would term a "one-world-island in a one-world-ocean". Fuller used the map for the end paper of his 1938 book *Nine Chains to the Moon*. Between 1938 and 1940, as technical advisor to *Fortune* magazine, Fuller deployed this map to demonstrate the increased mechanization of the U.S. with respect to the rest of the world, providing American citizens with a greater number of "energy slaves", or labour-saving machinery, than their counterparts elsewhere in the world.

The traditional Mercator projection, created in 1569 for an age of ocean-exploration, had the great advantage of translating a navigational route with a fixed compass bearing into a straight line. Fuller's map, designed for an age of long-distance flight, made the great circle polar air-routes visible and commensurable. In search of an easy technique for transferring great circles and coordinates from a globe to a flat surface while working for the Board of Economic Warfare in Washington D.C., Fuller came up with an ingenious method. He made a hemisphere out of transparent plastic. This could be placed over a globe, with the "equator" of the hemisphere being used to trace great circle routes between any two points. Fuller marked

Fuller with Dymaxion Air-Ocean Map, from *Life* magazine, vol. 14, no. 4, March 1, 1943

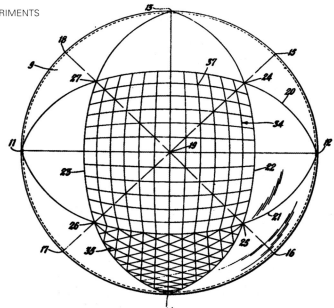

off eight equidistant points from the "equator", and joined diametrically opposite points with great circle lines (using the longitude lines of the underlying globe as a guide). All of these great circles crossed at one central point, corresponding to the North Pole of the plastic hemisphere. This produced a pattern that looked like the Union Jack. On four of these lines, Fuller then marked a point at 45° latitude between the equator and the North Pole. These points allowed him to trace four more great circles, producing a spherical square centered on the North Pole and four adjoining spherical triangles. Fuller then divided the spherical square and triangles into smaller square and triangular subdivisions, allowing him to read positions and geographical features from the globe and transfer them to a flat square and triangle of equal side-length. His technique for subdividing each triangle into smaller triangles was to mark points at equal intervals along each side and then trace great circles perpendicular to the sides. This technique would later be the basis of the so-called "regular grid" used in early geodesic dome design.

To map all of the features of the globe using Fuller's cartographic device generated a solid with six square faces and eight equilateral triangular faces. This solid, which Fuller immediately baptized with his trademark name, as the *Dymaxion*, was actually one of the semi-regular or Archimedean solids, normally called the cuboctahedron and known since antiquity. By mapping points on the surface of the globe in this way, Fuller produced a map of the world on the surface of a cuboctahedron. Two of the square faces of the cuboctahedron were centered on the North and South poles. One of the great circles formed where the tips of the triangular faces met was the equator. The solid could be opened out into a flat surface, or "polyhedral net", and recentered according to one's specific area of interest.

As with all systems for translating the globe onto a plane, Fuller's map involved distortions. However, in contrast to the "gnomonic projection" technique, that was normally used by cartographers for polyhedral projections (including in an icosahedral world map published in the same year as Fuller's map by Fisher and Miller), Fuller's map was most precise at the boundaries between cells, and most distorted at the centers of the cells. Gnomonic projections, which projected points from the center of the globe out onto a circumscribing polyhedron, were only orthogonal, and thereby accurate, at the centres of cells, and

Patent drawing of technique for creating
the Dymaxion Projection, 1946

Model cuboctahedron, also called a
Dymaxion and Vector Equilibrium by Fuller,
preserved in Stanford University Libraries.
Photograph: Stanford Visual Art Service

Celestial Dymaxion Map, showing the
constellations, undated

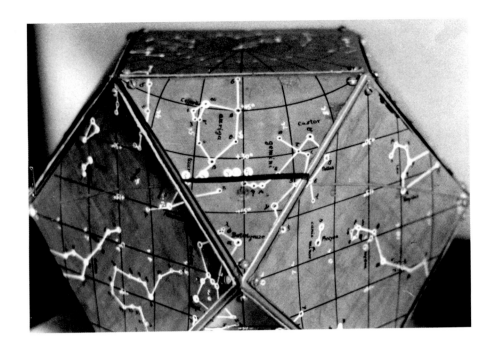

became gradually more distorted towards the boundaries.[35] In 1954, in collaboration with Shoji Sadao, Fuller published a revised icosahedral version of the *Dymaxion Air-Ocean Map* in Raleigh North Carolina. While it did not share the cuboctahedron's property of equal radius and edge length, the icosahedron was closer, in volume, to a sphere, and had the advantage of having identical triangular faces.

The concept of a polyhedral world map was not original to Fuller; indeed it can be traced back to Albrecht Dürer in his 1525 work *Underweysung der Messung*. The early twentieth century saw a number of polyhedral projections, including several octahedron-based maps by Bernard Cahill from 1909 on, using gnomonic, conformal or arbitrary projections, often arranged in the shape of a butterfly.

Fuller's cuboctahedral world map was published in a large pullout center spread in *Life* magazine in 1943, which attracted an enormous amount of attention. Cartographers criticized the Dymaxion Air-Ocean Map as "pure invention", as it was not, strictly speaking, a mathematical projection, but rather a rule-of thumb for transferring coordinates with the aid of great-circle grids, but, ironically, their criticisms actually helped Fuller to receive a patent for the map, as an invention, given that the patent office had ruled in 1900 that no further applications for world maps would be considered. An advantage of Fuller's world map (which it shared with gnomonic projections) was that great circles on the globe were represented as straight lines. In 1949 apparently without knowing about Fuller's Dymaxion Air-Ocean Map, M.C. Escher carried out a woodcut depicting a *Double Planetoid* shaped like a stella octangula, which he followed up in 1954 with a *Tetrahedral Planetoid*.

It is difficult to overstate the importance of Fuller's Dymaxion Air-Ocean Map for the development of his structural experiments from the 1940s on. As Krausse and Lichtenstein have written, the map "was a magnum opus for Fuller: the fundamentally important weigh station on the way to energetic-synergetic geometry and the geodesic domes"[36]. In the first place, the 1943 Dymaxion Air-Ocean Map introduced Fuller to the remarkable symmetry properties of the cuboctahedron and the geometry of the sphere. As the faces of the cuboctahedron were squares and equilateral triangles, every one of the edges of the solid had the same length. Moreover, if you joined the center of the cuboctahedron to each of its vertices, the

Dymaxion Projection Map displaying the
world distribution of "energy slaves"
(replacement of human labour by
machines), from Herbert Bayer,
World Geo-Graphic Atlas, 1953

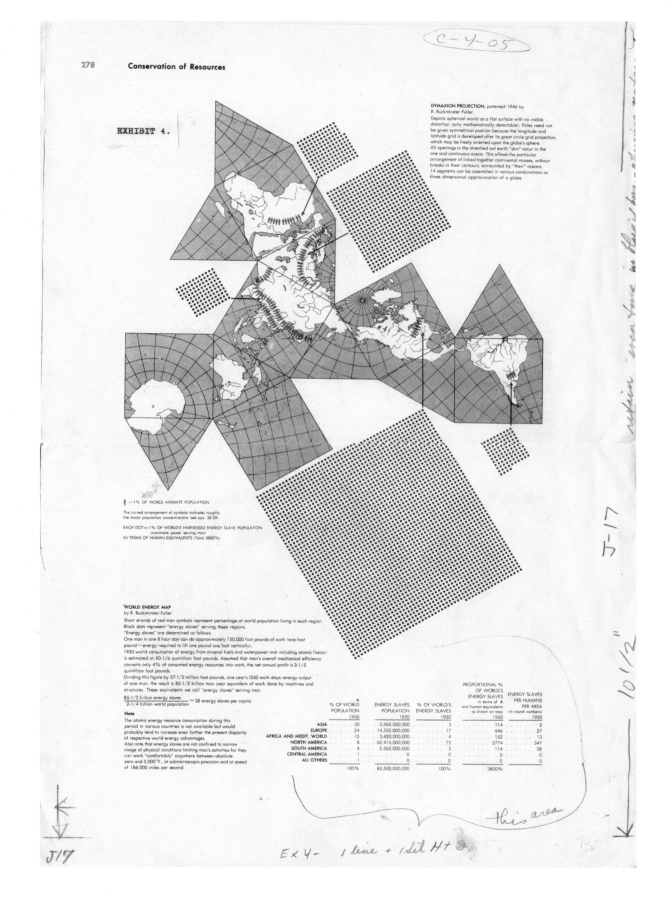

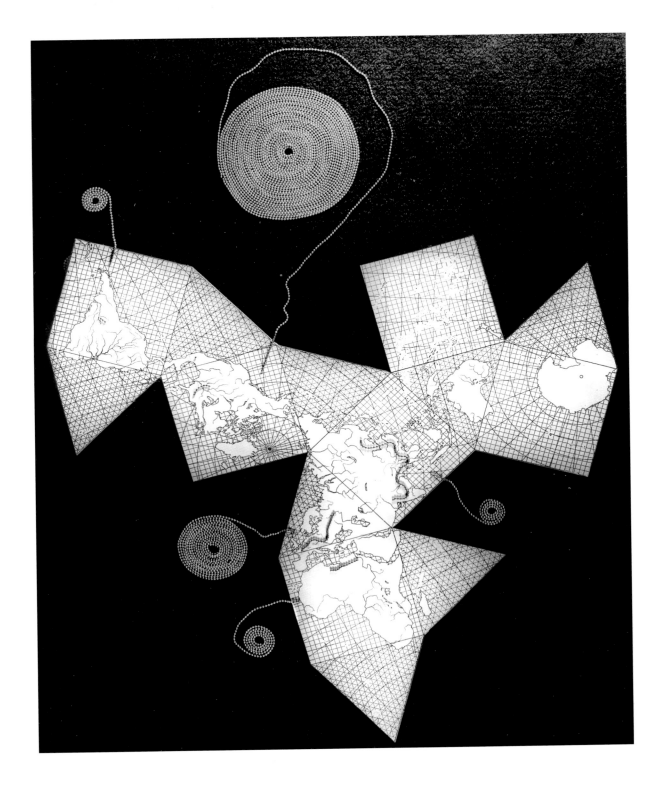

Another representation of the world
distribution of "energy slaves"

12 "radii" produced would have the same length as each of the edges. This unique property, experienced by creating several models, led Fuller to later call the cuboctahedron a "vector equilibrium", and he described the twelve radii connecting the center to each vertex as "twelve degrees of freedom". When the vertices of a cuboctahedron were joined to the center, a structure of enormous stability was produced, consisting of half-octahedra (or pyramids) with their bases on the square faces, and tetrahedra having bases on the triangular faces. The cuboctahedral shape of the 1943 Dymaxion Air-Ocean Map thus also gave Fuller a point of departure for his later investigations of the space-filling properties and structural stability of combinations of tetrahedra and octahedra.

The cuboctahedron can also be seen as being made up of four interlocking hexagonal planes. Fuller was already familiar with the structural advantages of the hexagon from his early Dymaxion House, so the prospect of four interlocking hexagons must have been especially exciting. The cuboctahedron, with its unique geometrical and structural properties, became something of a magic talisman for Fuller. Fuller explored the close packing of spheres into cuboctahedral layers, a phenomenon that had been studied by Kepler and formed the basis of the famous Kepler conjecture on face-centered cubic lattices.[37] Some of the results of Fuller's unorthodox investigations were met with disbelief by professional mathematicians. For example, Fuller claimed that the numbers of spheres in each successive close-packed layer – 12, 42, 92, 162 ... – were equal to the squares of the natural numbers followed by the numeral "2", a proposition met with disbelief by geometer H.S.M. Coxeter, to whom Fuller dedicated his magnum opus, *Synergetics*, until a formal proof was later produced by Arthur Loeb.

While hexagons could be used to tile the two-dimensional plane in a honeycomb pattern, the cuboctahedron alone could not be used to fill three-dimensional space. The cuboctahedron can be generated from a cube – which is space-filling – by "degenerate truncation". Take a cube, mark the midpoints

Energetic-synergetic geometry diagrams

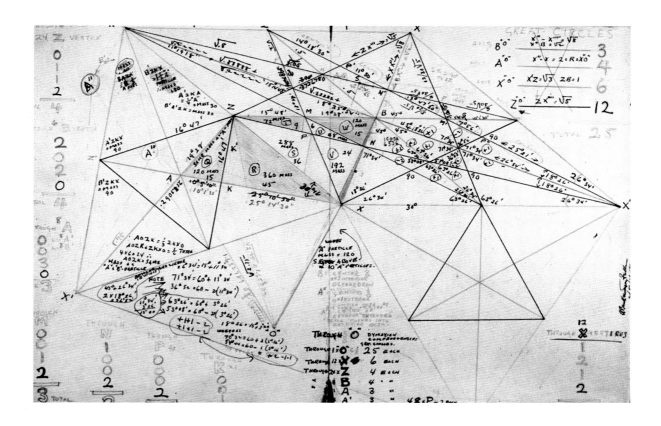

Diagrams demonstrating the close-packing
of spheres and synergetic geometry,
July 1948

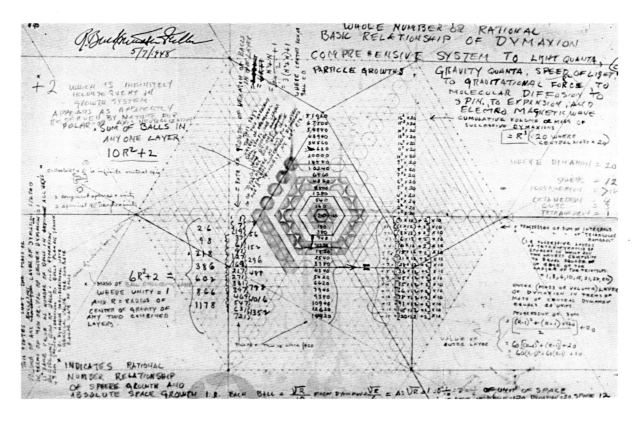

Model of the Isotropic Vector Matrix (IVM), made by Russell Chu, 1983. The model is preserved in Stanford University Libraries. Photograph: Stanford Visual Art Services

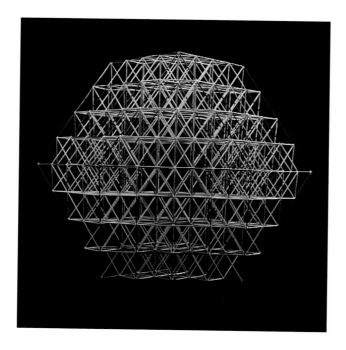

of each edge, join those points, and chop off the corners. You are left with a cuboctahedron and eight chopped-off tetrahedra. If you try to stack cuboctahedra together in three-dimensions, you will be left with an empty octahedron at each corner where eight cuboctahedra meet. Fuller called the space-filling structure generated by combining cuboctahedra (including the central node and radial struts) and octahedra in this way the Isotropic Vector Matrix (IVM). When Fuller hit upon this structure, he claimed he had discovered "the coordinates of Universe". His initial map experiments had driven him away from an essentially perpendicular conception of structure towards a three-dimensional coordinate grid with translational symmetry in twelve directions. The results of Fuller's investigations into what he called "energetic-synergetic geometry" were only published in two immense volumes, *Synergetics* and *Synergetics 2*, in 1975 and 1979 after a lengthy collaboration with Ed Applewhite and input from others including Harvard mathematician Arthur Loeb and physics and literature scholar Edwin Schlossberg. At Loeb's invitation, M.C. Escher had originally agreed to carry out the illustrations to the volumes, but unfortunately he died before their long and painful gestation period was over.

Fuller's geometrical researches in this period oscillated between the world of the very large – the geometry of the terrestrial globe and large-scale patterns of human activity – and the very small – the structural properties of molecules and crystals. In 1946, he established the Fuller Research Foundation in Forest Hills, New York, as a base for these fundamental investigations, as yet unconnected to any architectural application. His approach to mathematics was exploratory and experimental – the construction and manipulation of three-dimensional models was far more important than rigorous geometrical proofs. Although this approach alienated him from some professional mathematicians, it allowed Fuller to take shortcuts to some remarkable discoveries that a more rigorous approach would have precluded. Cardboard, toothpicks, rubber connectors, steel bands, ping-pong balls and marbles were the most important components of Fuller's geometrical toolbox. Great circles could be used, Fuller realized, to define a skeletal structure on the sphere with interesting geometric and structural properties.

Would the cuboctahedron of Fuller's 1943 Dymaxion Map be a suitable shape for a living space?

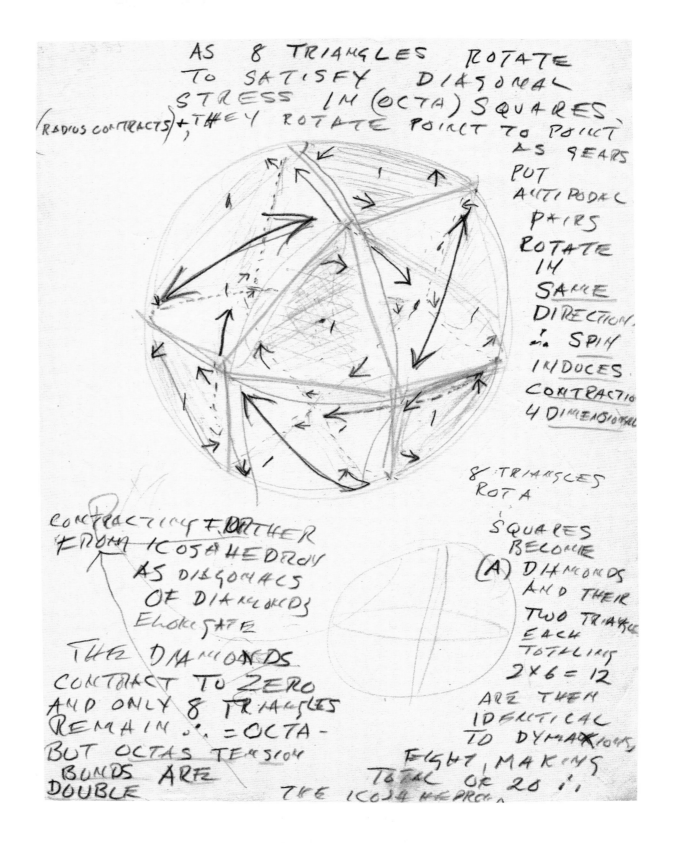

AS 8 TRIANGLES ROTATE
TO SATISFY DIAGONAL
STRESS IN (OCTA) SQUARES,
(RADIUS CONTRACTS) + THEY ROTATE POINT TO POINT
AS GEARS
PUT
ANTIPODAL
PAIRS
ROTATE
IN
SAME
DIRECTION
∴ SPIN
INDUCES
CONTRACTION
4 DIMENSIONAL

8 TRIANGLES
ROTA

SQUARES
BECOME
(A) DIAMONDS
AND THEIR
TWO TRIANGLE
EACH
TOTALING
2×6 = 12
ARE THEN
IDENTICAL
TO DYMAXIONS,
EIGHT, MAKING
TOTAL OF 20 ∴
THE ICOSAHEDRON

CONTRACTING FURTHER
FROM ICOSAHEDRON
AS DIAGONALS
OF DIAMONDS
ELONGATE

THE DIAMONDS
CONTRACT TO ZERO
AND ONLY 8 TRIANGLES
REMAIN ∴ = OCTA-
BUT OCTAS TENSION
BONDS ARE
DOUBLE

93

Geometrical studies of the cuboctahedron, inscribed in a cube and an octahedron, 1948

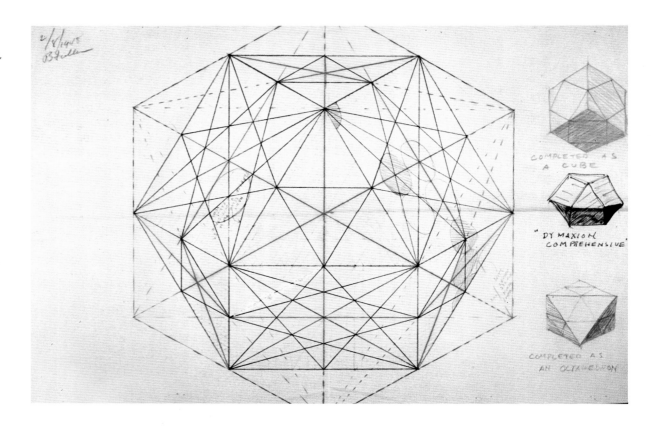

Unfortunately its extraordinary structural strength only comes into play when it is braced from the central node, thus dividing the space into awkward tetrahedral and half-octahedral cells. Without the central node being connected to all the vertices, the cuboctahedron is quite a flimsy and unstable structure. In fact, it was precisely this instability that attracted Fuller's interest in the late 1940s. He made model cuboctahedra with flexible rubber nodes. He noticed that when you pushed down on one of the triangular faces, the middle of the cuboctahedron twisted. The shape passed through distinct phases – first, the vertices defined a regular icosahedron, then, as you pushed further, it collapsed into a regular octahedron. When the top triangle was now twisted, the entire system collapsed into a flat triangle. By folding in the three-corner triangles, you could produce a tetrahedron, what Fuller called the "minimum system of Universe". If you let go of the tetrahedron, it would spring back into the original cuboctahedral form. The twisting motion of the cuboctahedron could occur in both directions. Fuller named this twisting geometrical dance the *Jitterbug Transformation*.

He believed that the "phase transitions" between different solids (cuboctahedron, icosahedron, octahedron and tetrahedron) were of fundamental physical importance. When he arrived at the transformation sequence in April 1948, Fuller wrote ecstatically in his notebook "*Eureka – Eureka – and Eureka again!!! This is what Archimedes sought and Pythagoras and Kepler and Newton*"[38]. His elation is reminiscent of the joy of his hero Johannes Kepler on "discovering" that the planetary orbits appeared to fit into the nested Platonic solids, quoted by Edgar Allen Poe: "I care not whether my work be read now or by posterity. I can afford to wait a century for readers when God himself has waited six thousand years for an observer. I triumph. I have stolen the golden secret of the Egyptians. I will indulge my sacred fury"[39]. The Jitterbug transformation, a clear consequence of Fuller's hands-on approach to mathematical demonstration, became a set piece in Fuller's public lectures although some questioned its physical significance.

Early study of great-circle grid on spherical icosahedron, undated

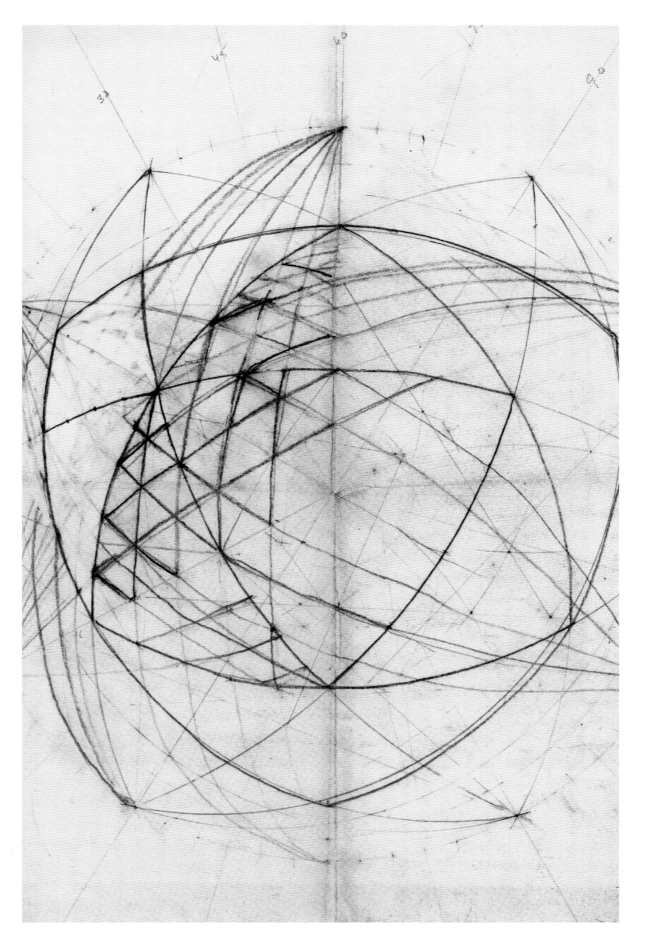

31-great circle grid on a spherical icosahedron. This was the first grid-system used by Fuller, but the resultant structure was not physically stable due to the large differences in strut length

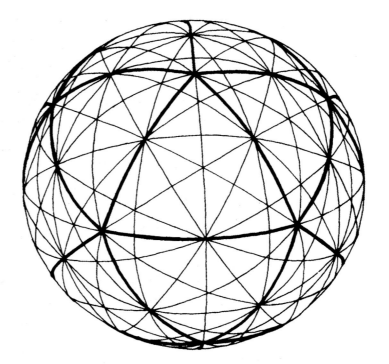

The simple great circle tool (a transparent hemisphere designed to fit snugly over a globe) that had assisted Fuller in creating the 1943 Dymaxion Map projection could also be used to scribe a sphere with great circles corresponding to other regular and semi-regular solids. In the revised version of the Dymaxion Map published by Fuller and Sadao in 1954, the sphere was divided up into an icosahedral grid, rather than the cuboctahedral grid of 1943. Fuller's shift from the analysis of cuboctahedral grids to icosahedral grids, which contained identical triangular faces, between 1943 and 1954 was connected to the development of his most famous architectural structure, the geodesic dome.

While the available documents do not tell us the whole story, it seems likely that Fuller's road to the geodesic dome was, first, through the inscription of regular solids onto the sphere (using the great circle methods developed for the 1943 map), then, through the construction of great circle models that allowed him to experience the structural stability of triangulated geodesic structures at first hand, and finally through the conception of great-circle architectural structures. The geodesic dome emerged in its final form through the development of the concept of "frequency", again derived from his work subdividing faces of spherical solids in the Dymaxion Map.

All of these developments appear to have occurred very quickly between 1948 and 1950, the year in which Fuller's first successful geodesic dome based on an icosahedral net was erected near Montreal. In the Spring of 1948, Fuller had developed a hemispherical great circle model incorporating the thirty-one great circles derived from the rotational symmetries of the spherical icosahedron. Around the same time he made a sketch of a possible architectural application, entitled *Your Private Sky*. This device was something like a personal planetarium. It consisted of a great-circle dome. The great circles, enhanced with elements of a star-map, allowed the inhabitant to perform accurate celestial observations and "see his geography correctly", by observing the position of the North star, and so on. Fuller even suggested that a hemispherical swimming pool could be decorated with the antipodean constellations, allowing the inhabitant to contemplate the cosmic order while floating in the water.

Fuller with geometric models at Black
Mountain College, 1948

Fuller using the 31-great-circle hemisphere as a model for the unsuccessful "Supine Dome" with students from Black Mountain College, 1948

Great-circle model, circa 1949

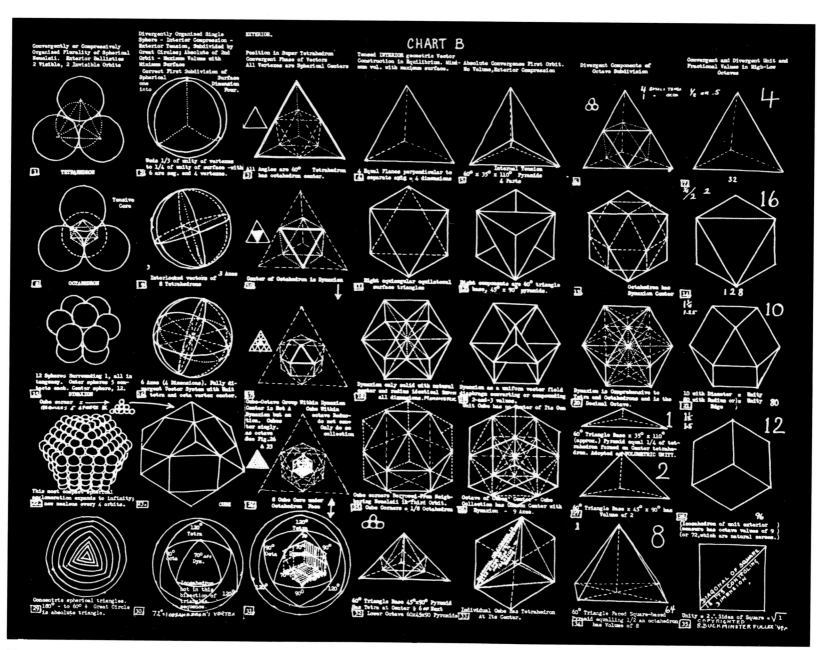

Diagram depicting the principles of
energetic-synergetic geometry, undated

Fuller's combination of celestial map and living space demonstrates the striking convergence between mapping the globe and designing lightweight structures that characterized the evolution of the geodesic dome, a convergence that was later demonstrated in his 1952 Geoscope project at Cornell University, where a terrestrial map was overlaid on a geodesic sphere.[40] Interestingly the first known triangulated geodesic dome, predating Fuller's extensive research, was produced for a planetarium, the Zeiss planetarium in Jena, by Walter Bauersfeld in 1922, and his use of an icosahedral structure followed from a desire to project celestial maps accurately.

Fuller experimented with the symmetrical figures that could be created by tracing great circles onto the sphere. Building initial wire models, he noted that the more great circles were present, the stronger the model. These great circles are the "equators" formed when the icosahedron is rotated about an axis joining polar-opposite points (vertices, midpoints of edges and centres of faces). Fuller termed these polar-opposite points "poles of spinnability", again indicating his "hands-on" approach to geometry – physicists balked at his suggestions of a connection with the quantum-mechanical concept of "spin".

As the spherical icosahedron has twelve vertices, twenty faces, and thirty edges, it generates 6 + 10 + 15 = 31 great circles, the largest number possible for any regular or semi-regular solid. The cuboctahedron, by way of comparison, in spite of its magical quality of equal radius and edge length, generates only 25.

The icosahedron, with its twenty equilateral triangle faces, is the basis of the vast majority of geodesic domes. A few are derived from the "dual" of the icosahedron, the dodecahedron, with its twelve pentagonal faces, which can be made by joining the centers of the faces of the icosahedron. Some domes, like the early Wood's Hole Restaurant and wooden Aspen domes of 1953, are derived from the 30-faced rhombic triacontahedron, which is the dual of the solid formed through the combination of an icosahedron and dodecahedron, the icosadodecahedron. This group (icosahedron, pentagonal dodecahedron and rhombic triacontahedron) forms a small family of solids, all of which have underlying five-fold symmetry.

When the triangular faces of the spherical icosahedron are subdivided into smaller triangles, in

Students at the Chicago Institute of Design
with the Standard of Living Package model,
1949

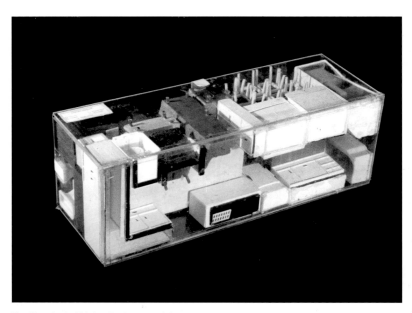

The Standard of Living Package model,
Chicago Institute of Design, 1948

Model installation of Standard of Living
Package, 1948

The Standard of Living Package model, 1949

The Standard of Living Package model, Chicago Institute of Design, 1948

exactly the way that Fuller had subdivided the triangular faces of the 1943 Dymaxion map, the following pattern can be observed: around every vertex of the original icosahedron, there are five triangles, making up a spherical pentagon. Around every other node, there are six triangles, making up a spherical hexagon. Almost every geodesic dome can be seen to consist of this mixture of hexagons and pentagons.

An icosahedral geodesic dome extended around to become a sphere always has exactly twelve pentagons, corresponding to the twelve vertices of the icosahedron. The five-fold symmetry of geodesic domes is one of their most distinctive characteristics. The number of subdivisions of each edge of one of the twenty equilateral triangular faces of the original icosahedron is termed the "frequency" of the dome. For example, if the edge of a triangle is divided into four struts, the dome is said to have a frequency of four. If the triangular faces of the icosahedron were planar, the triangular subdivisions would all have equal side-length. However, the nodes of the triangle, including the nodes of the subdivisions, all occupy the surface of a sphere. The struts connecting nodes are thus chords of a segment of a great circle, and do not have equal length. The calculation of the length of these struts is done by means of so-called "chord factors" derived using spherical trigonometry.[41]

When Fuller arrived in his streamlined Airstream trailer to teach in Black Mountain College in North Carolina in Summer 1948, he brought his semicircular icosahedral great circle model with him, among many other models and demonstration tools developed in New York. Black Mountain College was an extraordinary educational experiment, commingling artists, scientists, architects and writers, and it was there, in the Summers of 1948 and 1949, that Fuller came into close contact with Joseph and Anni Albers, John Cage, Merce Cunningham, Ruth Asawa, Kenneth Snelson, Arthur Penn, Willem and Elaine de Kooning and Robert Rauschenberg. Immediately after he arrived, Fuller delivered a three-hour lecture explain-

ing his recent geometrical experiments, brandishing a remarkable array of tetrahedra, closely packed spheres and the recently discovered jitterbug transformation, which apparently had an electrifying effect on many members of the audience.

Shortly afterwards, Fuller enlisted the help of many of the Black Mountain College students to create a first large version of a geodesic structure. This structure was to be a large great circle dome, modelled directly on the thirty-one great circle hemisphere model that Fuller used as a blueprint and actually brought into the field where the dome was to be erected. The struts were the metal slats from Venetian blinds, and were not rigid, because Fuller wanted them to follow great circle lines directly (in contrast with his subsequent geodesic domes which were made up of straight, rigid struts constituting *chords* of great circles – a key transition). Fuller later claimed, in his priority dispute with Kenneth Snelson over tensegrity structures, that he tried using short wooden slats as chords to help give the slack, ribbony dome shape, but ran out of slats (Albert Lanier's eyewitness account of the occasion does not make any mention of the wooden slats). In spite of the help of many students, the 48-foot dome resolutely refused to stand up, leading to it being nicknamed the "Supine Dome". Fuller blamed the poor materials for the failed dome, but in fact the failure may have spurred him to develop the successful model manifested in Jeffrey Lindsay's 1950 Montreal Dome.

Unperturbed by the failure, Fuller availed of a teaching stint at the Institute of Design in Chica-

Fuller with Standard Living Package and
Skybreak Dome model, 1949

Necklace Dome, Black Mountain College,
1949

Fuller emerging from the Necklace Dome,
1949

go that Autumn to assign his students the problem of making all the furnishings that would be required by a family of six people so that they could be packed into a trailer.

They came up with the *Standard of Living Package*, a container whose sides folded down to make a floor, including all standard household furnishings. Fuller conceived the Standard of Living Package as a complementary project to the geodesic dome, designed to provide a portable living environment. During the same period he also developed a more practical solution for connecting his struts. This consisted of rigid metal tubes, threaded together on a string, giving rise to the nickname "Necklace Dome". The dome used the same thirty-one great circle pattern used in the Supine Dome to grid the icosahedron. Appropriately, given its rich pentagonal symmetries, the *Necklace Dome* was first constructed and exhibited in the gardens of the Pentagon in Washington D.C. in February 1949, inaugurating a blossoming romance between the geodesic dome and the U.S. military.

In the Summer of 1949, Fuller returned to Black Mountain College, bringing with him his design students from Chicago (whose cult-like adulation of Fuller was reportedly a source of disgruntlement to some of the other students). There, they installed the Necklace Dome, covering it in a skin of transparent plastic. As the struts in the Necklace Dome were straight, and thus chords, rather than curved great-circle arcs, it represented a halfway house between the "Supine Dome" and the Montreal Dome of 1950. According to Fuller's collaborator Don Richter, one of the problems of the Necklace Dome was that wherever only two struts crossed, the structure was unstable, and could even be pushed inward to produce a concave or "involute" structure. The fundamental difference between the 1949 Necklace Dome and the 1950

Montreal Dome, is in the way the triangular faces of the icosahedron were subdivided into a grid in each case. In the case of the Necklace Dome, all of the great circles defined by the poles of rotational symmetry of the icosahedron were traced, and their intersections were marked as nodes. In the case of the Montreal Dome of 1950, each individual triangular facet of the spherical icosahedron was subdivided into a number of smaller spherical triangles by marking off points at equal intervals along each edge of the triangle, and then using great circle arcs to draw perpendiculars, using exactly the same technique used in the Dymaxion Map construction, the so-called "regular grid". The length used for the struts was then equal to the chord of the great circle arc between two neighbouring nodes, and would differ for different frequency domes. The dome was designed and constructed by Jeffrey Lindsay with the assistance of Don Richter, who had been Fuller's students at the Chicago Institute of Design. In the Summer of 1950 Fuller had written a privately circulated manuscript entitled *Noah's Ark # 2*, in which he described a clever practical technique for measuring strut-lengths using an equilateral triangle made of three bands of spring-steel punched at equal intervals along their length.[42]

The Montreal Dome of 1950, using the grid of the Dymaxion Air-Ocean Map, represented a solution that more closely approximated equilateral triangles with nodes occupying the surface of a sphere. It was extremely light (made from aluminium tubes) and remarkably strong. Short, stubby poles, or "sprits" radiating out from each node carried tension wires to add stiffness to the structure, and a fabric skin was stretched under the frame. The problem with the grid technique used – the "regular grid" – was that it generally left "windows". It proved impossible to get struts to meet precisely at the vertices, despite the best efforts of Fuller and his assistants, with the aid of trigonometry tables and mechanical calculators. This led to the development of several other grid systems. The "alternate grid" was created by taking the midpoints of each edge of a triangular face and joining them, thus producing four smaller triangles. The process could be iterated on each of the smaller triangles as many times as required. The lengths of struts were easier to calculate mathematically for the alternate grid than for the regular grid, and there were fewer struts of different-lengths, cutting costs. A third grid design, the "triacon grid", discovered by Duncan Stuart, involved using the diamonds generated by the thirty-one great circle sphere, rather than the triangular icosahedral faces, as the unit to be subdivided. This grid removed the problem of "windows" experienced for the regular grid, and proved extremely popular in geodesic dome design.

In some geodesic domes, including the radomes produced to house radar along the Distant Early Warning (DEW) line, more than a hemisphere was required. In this case, it was necessary to find a way to truncate the dome below the equator, but still have all of the vertices fall on a single line. Clearly this line would have to be a "line of latitude" of the dome, parallel to the equator. Bill Wainwright of the Cambridge office of Fuller's company Geodesics Inc. devised the "parallel grid" to deal with this situation.[43]

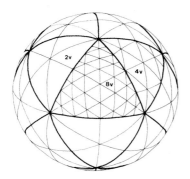

The regular grid used in construction of the first geodesic domes

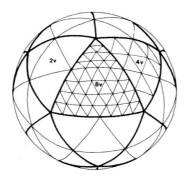

The alternate grid. Subdivisions of just one triangle of the spherical icosahedron are shown

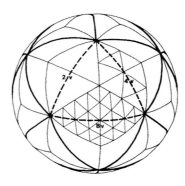

The triacon grid, discovered by Duncan Stuart in 1951

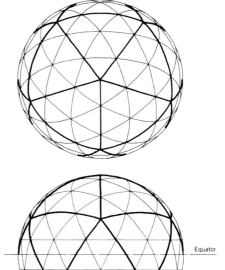

The truncatable or parallel grid, devised by Bill Wainwright

[35] Irving Fisher, "A World Map on a Regular Icosahedron by Gnomonic Projection", *The Geographical Review*, 33, 4: 605-619, (1943).
[36] Joachim Krausse and Claude Lichtenstein, eds., *Your Private Sky: R. Buckminster Fuller The Art of Design Science*, Lars Müller, Zürich, 1999, p. 250.
[37] N.J.A. Sloane, "Kepler's Conjecture Confirmed", *Nature*, no. 395, pp. 435-436, 1998.
[38] Krausse and Lichtenstein, eds., *Your Private Sky*, cit., p. 291.

[39] Poe, *Eureka: A Prose Poem*, 1848, quoted in E.J. Applewhite, *Cosmic Fishing. An Account of Writing Synergetics with Buckminster Fuller*, Macmillan, New York, 1977, and Hugh Kenner, *Bucky: A Guided Tour of Buckminster Fuller*, William Morrow, New York, 1973.
[40] Krausse and Lichtenstein, eds., *Your Private Sky*, cit., pp. 346-7.
[41] For details, see Amy C. Edmondson, *A Fuller Explanation* and Hugh Kenner, *Geodesic Math and How to Use it*, University of California Press,

Berkeley, 1976.
[42] *Noah's Ark #2*, published in Joachim Krausse and Claude Lichtenstein, eds., *Your Private Sky: Discourse*, Lars Müller, Zürich, 2001, pp. 176-225.
[43] Shoji Sadao, *A Brief History of Geodesic Domes*, in Thomas T.K. Zung, ed., *Buckminster Fuller: Anthology for the New Millenium*, St. Martins Press, New York, 2001, pp. 19-28.

Skybreak Dome model, 1949

Model of Skybreak dwelling including
Standard of Living Package, 1948

The 49-foot diameter Montreal Geodesic
Dome built by the Fuller Research
Foundation, Canadian division, in December
1950. The project was carried out in Canada

due to the continued rationing of aluminium
in the U.S.
Note the "sprits" projecting outwards from
the nodes, connected by tension wires

A break during construction of the Montreal
Geodesic Dome, December 1950

Great-circle models

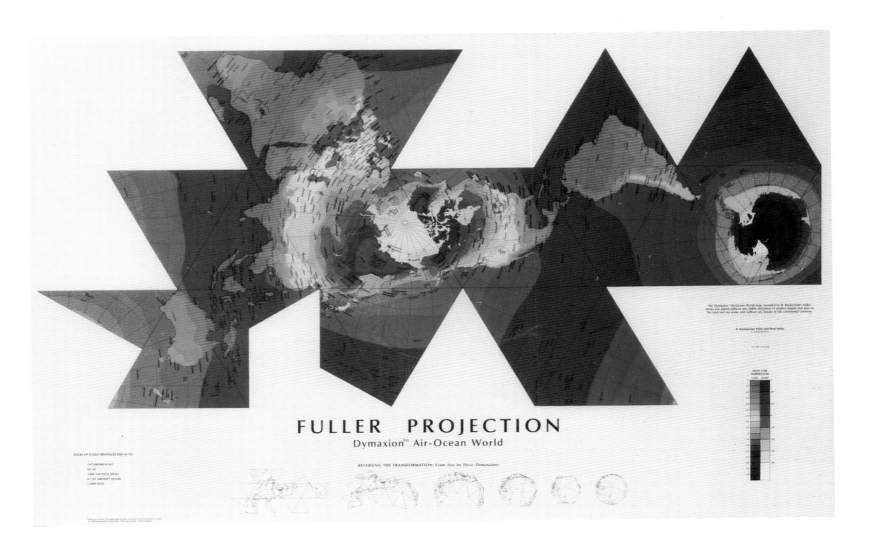

FULLER PROJECTION

Dymaxion™ Air-Ocean World

6. The Geodesic Dome

The geodesic dome, which would catapult R. Buckminster Fuller into worldwide fame, represented a distinct departure from his previous designs for living spaces. Where the 4D Towers, Dymaxion House and Wichita Dwelling Machine had all been suspended from a central mast, the geodesic dome had no central mast, no privileged vertical axis of symmetry. In building the Wichita House, Fuller noted that it was necessary to incorporate stays to block the mast from being overturned by the wind, and ultimately the stays took up a large portion of the living area. As Fuller wrote, introducing the 1954 patent for the geodesic dome, "it became a spherical mast". The dome redistributed local impact stresses to all structural members.

While Fuller's previous building-conceptions generally had an "endoskeleton" housing a "central nervous system", like a human being, geodesic domes had an "exoskeleton", like a sea urchin or an egg. This was an architectural structure that drew inspiration from the very large – consideration of the terrestrial and celestial spheres – and the very small – microorganisms and radiolaria. In his explorations of synergetic geometry, from the 1940s on, Fuller truly believed that he was investigating "nature's own coordinate system", inspired by the plates of Ernst Haeckel's *Kunstformen der Natur* and D'Arcy Thompson's *On Growth and Form*. Fuller's geodesic domes defied the vertical axis, in the same way that in conversation he refused to acknowledge "up" and "down" as genuine linguistic distinctions, preferring "inward" and "outward", with respect to the earth's centre. For the aquatic microstructures in which Fuller saw echoes of his structures, gravitation did not play a significant role in constraining physical development. On the global scale, a radial view of gravitation was more appropriate than a linear view. Fuller's audacity was in importing such a radial approach to structure into the intermediate realm inhabited by humans, birds and trees, where, in spite of the best efforts of his friend Roger Babson, one vertical gravitational axis does tend to predominate.

The geodesic dome did not emerge from an analysis of the bracing problems inherent in the Wichita House – rather, as we have suggested, it evolved through a complex process from a cartographic problem and the dexterous manipulation of very simple devices – a transparent plastic hemisphere fitted closely over the surface of a globe, and a spring-steel triangle punched with holes. Nonetheless Fuller's assessment of its "synergetic" structural properties is concise and accurate. In June 1970, when offering Fuller its much coveted gold-medal, the American Institute of Architects acclaimed the geodesic dome as "the strongest, lightest and most efficient means of enclosing space yet known to man"[44].

In some ways, Fuller was a victim of the extraordinary success of the geodesic dome, reflected in his dizzying lecture schedule and rapidly multiplying invitations for visiting professorships in the years following 1948. His philosophy of the home, expounded in *4D Timelock* and developed in his 1929 Dymax-

Fuller with a geodesic sphere model

Drawing from patent application for
geodesic dome, 1954

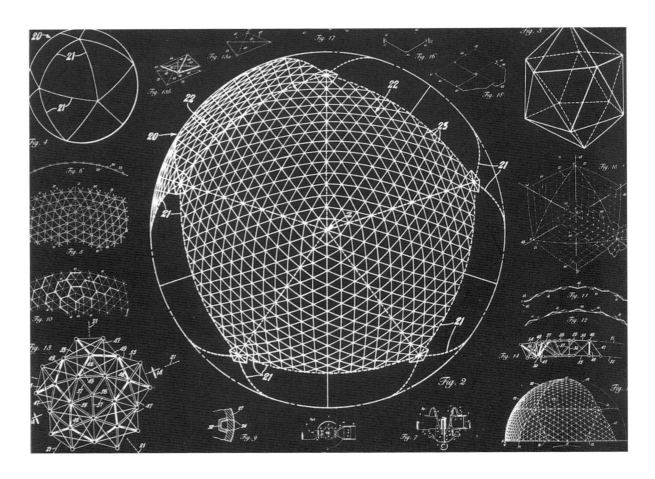

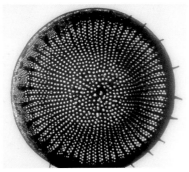

Radiolarian structure

ion House, was very much a systems philosophy, which included certain crucial elements: industrial fabri-
cation, air-delivery, and intellectual and practical autonomy. With the development of the geodesic dome,
Fuller was associated with a new kind of structure, a shell eviscerated of its philosophical yolk, and ready
to be invested with widely varying ideologies and stuffed with all manner of physical artifacts ranging from
military radar antennae to helicopters, Disney rides, Whirlpool kitchen units and hallucinating hippies.
Amidst the noise of the many ideologies clamouring to appropriate the geodesic dome as both a practical
solution and symbol, Fuller's own voice had to be amplified to be heard.

To describe Fuller as a passive victim of the success of the dome would be naive, however – Fuller
was rather adept at manipulating his newfound fame. Speaker fees for invited lectures and stipends for visiting professorships provided Fuller with a crucial source of income, which supported his ongoing projects.
Perhaps even more innovative was the way he used universities as his own, decentralized R&D laboratories.
When Fuller was invited to MIT, North Carolina State, and other universities, he usually came with a specific project in mind. He would use his notorious "marathon" lectures to galvanize large numbers of students into working for him, with all materials and expenses subsidized by the university, which also provided
its best workshops and technicians. In this way, Fuller could use universities as experimental testing grounds,
and have access to some of the best young talent available for free. He was careful to protect himself from
universities appropriating his intellectual property, and obliged them to waive normal "shop rights". Students were also obliged to sign forms crediting Fuller with any discoveries made as a consequence of their
work with him. Generally, the strategy worked well – the students had the inspiring experience of working
on the cutting edge of a research project, and the intellectual property issues only occasionally generated

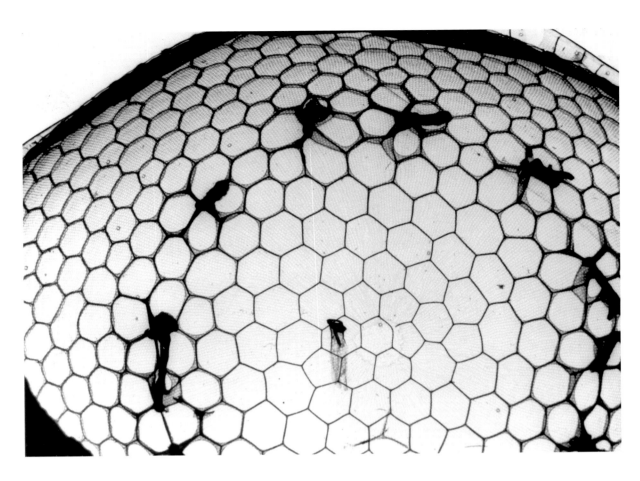

friction, when students were surprised that Fuller did not credit them for their discoveries. One college dean remarked that "many of the students will fully reject all other teaching they have had in your school because of their experiences with him, and I think you had better expect that"[45]. Fuller's strategic use of universities echoed his use of the resources of the U.S. military to develop his projects.

Fuller's approach to intellectual property, rather than being a personal foible, as some have suggested, is, I want to argue, a key to understanding the locus of his career. In contrast to the vast majority of architects, Fuller was a firm believer in the patent as the tool of progress in the building industry. At the same time Fuller was both an "inventor" of new built forms and someone who believed he was revealing nature's own geometry in both his buildings and his geometrical experiments. It is impossible to patent a law of nature or a mathematical proof, so Fuller's structural work occupies a dangerous no-man's land between the revelation of nature and the invention of structures. Fuller got around the problem through his notion of "synergy": "One cannot patent geometry per se nor any separate differentiated out, pure principle of nature's operative processes. One can patent, however, the surprise complex behaviours of associated principles, where the behaviour of the whole is unpredicted by the behaviour of the parts, i.e. synergetic phenomena". In response to those who suggested that his geodesic structures were merely "citations" of natural forms such as those illustrated by Haeckel and D'Arcy Thompson, Fuller retorted that: "Though superficially similar in patternings to Radiolaria and Fly's Eyes, geodesic structuring is true invention. The Radiolaria collapse when taken out of water. Fly's Eyes will not provide structural precedent or man-occupiable structures"[46].

Simply put, one could not live inside a fly's eye or a radiolarian, therefore geodesic domes were

Electron micrograph of radiolarian structure

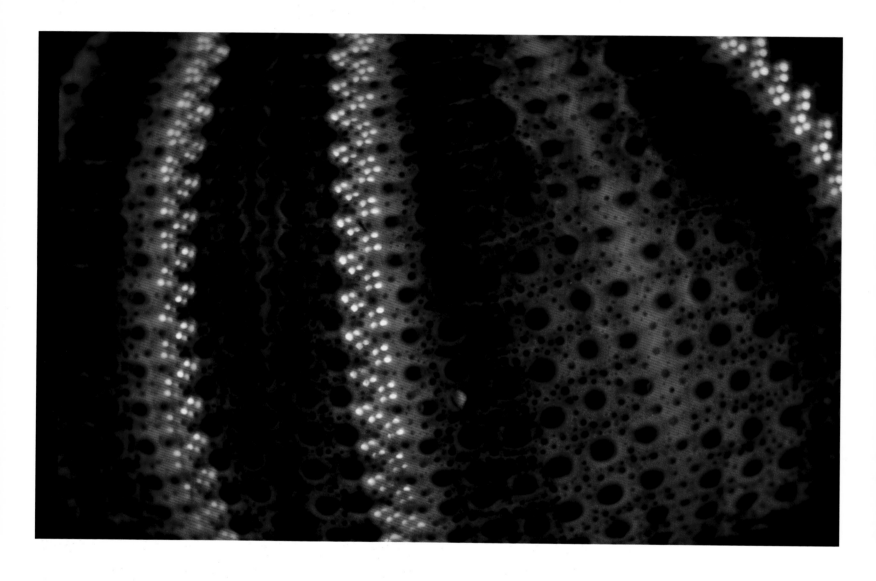

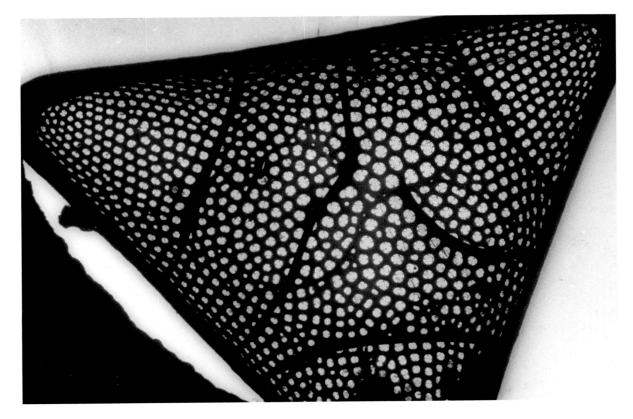

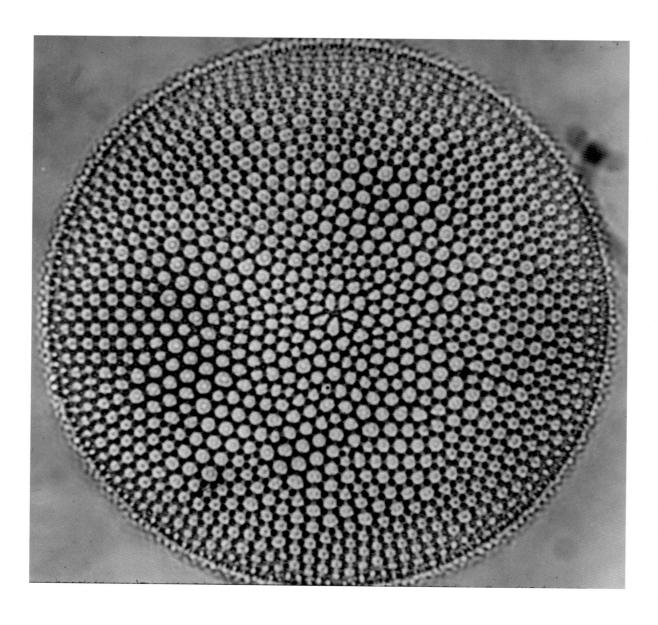

Sketches of colour-coding system for dome, circa 1953

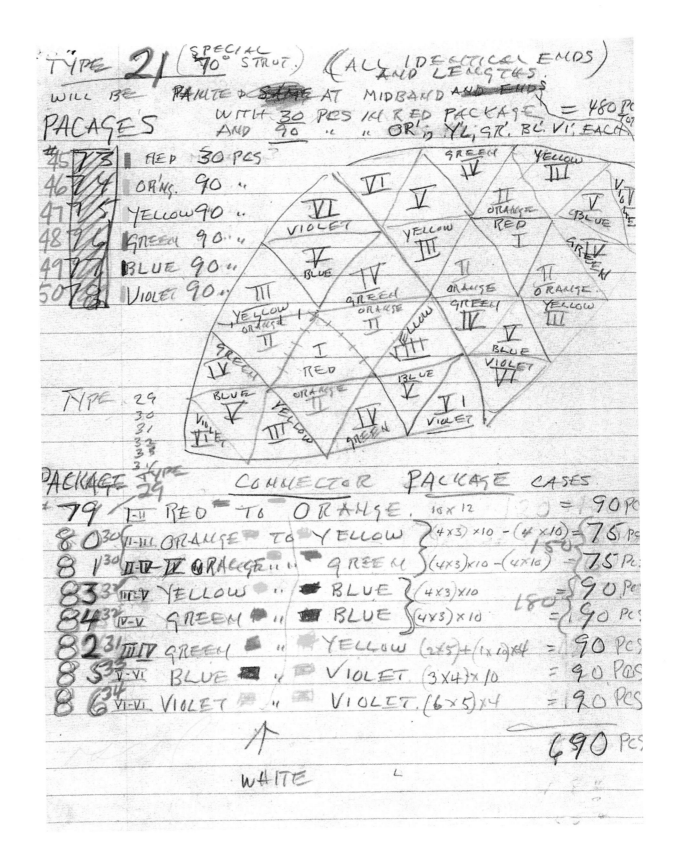

Project for a 90% automated cotton mill,
North Carolina State College, 1951

inventions rather than merely revelations of phenomena present in nature – an argument that it is difficult to refute. Fuller's approach to intellectual property, while it certainly set him apart from architects and scientists of his time, was rationalized to the extreme. If he was going to reveal his new discoveries to thousands of students, he needed to be protected from them developing his hard-earned results for their own ends. Similarly, the fact that his inventions were simultaneously profound demonstrations of the forces acting in nature in no way precluded them from being his intellectual property.

As the potential for using geodesic domes to create large clear-span structures economically became clear, Fuller's domes were invested with a range of functions going far beyond the domestic functions on which he had concentrated in the early part of his career.

A project with North Carolina State College, launched in 1951 and completed in January 1952 aimed to produce a geodesic cotton-mill.

One of the challenges in designing the cotton-mill was to develop a flooring-structure capable of supporting 200 pounds per square foot. This was accomplished through use of grids consisting of combinations of octahedra and tetrahedra. The fundamental unit of this structure was what Fuller called the *Octet Truss*. When grids made up of octet-truss units were stacked on top of one another, they produced the space-filling "Isotropic Vector Matrix". Due to its triangulated nature, the octet truss had remarkable resistance to compression. In 1953, Fuller tested an Octet Truss made of 170 aluminium struts at the University of Michigan. Although the entire frame weighed only 65 pounds, it could support six tons, the weight of a small army tank.

Octet Truss structure extended into grids to make flooring for a 90% automated cotton mill, North Carolina State College, 1951

Project for a 90% automated cotton mill, North Carolina State College, 1951

Fuller with the model of the geodesic dome commissioned by the Ford Motor Company for its Rotunda building at Dearborn, Michigan, 1953

Fuller patented the Octet Truss in 1961, as a structure suitable for roof and floor structures. Many years previously, in 1907, Alexander Graham Bell had experimented with exactly the same truss structure in designing kites and even building a seventy foot high tetrahedral observation tower that was described in National Geographic. In response to the claim that Bell had anticipated his octet truss, Fuller recalled creating an octet-truss in kindergarten using toothpicks and semi-dried peas in 1899, an unusual priority claim that he backed up with a testimony from his kindergarten teacher written fifty-years after the event, although other versions of the story have the intuitive infant R. Buckminster Fuller creating a tetrahedron or even a cuboctahedron from his toothpicks and peas.

Fuller's first major commission for a geodesic dome came from "Mr. Industry himself", when the Ford Motor Company commissioned a 93-foot geodesic dome over its Rotunda at Dearborn, Michigan in 1952. The gear-shaped Rotunda had been designed by Albert Kahn for the 1933 Chicago Worlds' Fair and moved to the Ford headquarters in Michigan. Don Richter offered Fuller advice on negotiating building codes, by defining the dome as a "skylight" rather than a roofing structure. Waterproofing the large dome proved to be very difficult, a problem that would dog the geodesic dome for many years to come, given the challenges in sealing a multi-faceted, multi-jointed structure. Initially the dome was to be covered with polyester fibreglass, but this could not be made in time, so in the end the dome was covered with a vinyl skin, and it leaked.

The years following 1952 saw a profusion of different dome projects, carried out by Fuller and others. In 1953 a geodesic dome restaurant was built at Wood's Hole, Massachusetts using a rhombic tria-

The Ford Dearborn Rotunda, with Fuller's dome in place, 1953

contrahedral design with the aid of students from the MIT graduate school of architecture. Because of its tightly stretched Mylar skin, the dome amplified conversations and music in the restaurant, working as a giant loudspeaker and irritating distant neighbours. The MIT student who had built the first wooden geodesic dome, Zane Yost, also worked with Fuller and Shoji Sadao on developing a paperboard dome. Exhibited at the X Triennale di Milano in 1954, the paperboard dome was awarded a Gran Premio of the Triennale, despite not being an official entry. Because of the lack of paperboard with sufficient wet tensile strength, the dome had to be coated in vinyl, aluminium foil and other materials.

In addition to their many civilian uses, Fuller's geodesic domes rapidly attracted the attention of the U.S. military in the aftermath of the Korean war. As Alex Pang has demonstrated, the domes were presented by Fuller to the military as a "double-barrelled geodesic weapon" with which they could gain competitive edge in both hot and cold wars. Pre-assembled, airlifted domes could be dropped into a war-zone in the third world at the outbreak of a "brush-fire war", to provide "environment controls" including housing, maintenance facilities and hangars for air force and marines at the first sign of Communist insurgence. "The side which has the superior environment controls will win", Fuller argued in an extraordinary 1956 letter to Major George King.[47] Early airlifting experiments, from the 1954 airlift in Raleigh, North Carolina to a subsequent demonstration at the Philadelphia air show, were encouraging. While the purposes of these demonstrations were a long way removed from mass-produced civilian domestic spaces, Fuller had been keenly aware since his navy days that the military had the vast resources to support advanced technological research that only later trickled down for the benefit of the civilian population. Fuller's notion of

125

Rhombic triacontrahedral dome

the geodesic dome as "environment control" harks back to his investigations of the thermodynamic properties of the Butler Dymaxion Dwelling Unit. Geodesic domes could be used to create a serviceable microclimate even in the harshest external conditions.

Another key project of this time in which the ability of geodesic domes to stand up to harsh climates was paramount was the development of the *Distant Early Warning (DEW) Line* in the mid 1950s. This project aimed to give the U.S. advance notice of an air-attack approaching it's Arctic border through radar stations positioned along a line about 200 miles North of the Arctic circle in Alaska and Northern Canada. Between 1954 and 1957, with the aid of Bill Wainwright and MIT's Lincoln Lab, Fuller developed the "radomes", designed to protect delicate radar from the extremely harsh weather conditions in a non-metallic structure. The project was carried out by Western Electric, under management of AT&T, and involved transporting 460,000 tons of material to the Arctic, by air, land and water.

The Geodesic Dome was thus both an offensive weapon, to be used in winning brush-fire wars, and a key component in U.S. defense from a Russian air strike, in the years just before Sputnik. To deal with the ever-increasing number of contracts for geodesic domes, Fuller founded two firms, Geodesics Inc. for military and government contracts, and Synergetics Inc. for civilian/industry contracts. In addition to direct military use, in the late 1950s the Geodesic Dome showed that it was also a valuable rhetorical tool in demonstrating the superiority of U.S.-style capitalism and democracy, together constituting the "synergetic strength of the USA" over communism.

In 1956, the Office of International Trade Fairs invited Fuller's firm Geodesics Inc. to create a prefabricated building for the trade fair in Kabul, Afghanistan. The designs for the 100-foot diameter dome were produced in only a week, and the dome was flown from America to Afghanistan in one DC-4 plane. The dome parts were colour-coded, so that untrained workmen with any native language could erect it. Within fortyheight hours, the dome – 100 feet in diameter – had been erected by local Afghan workmen, who were instantly acclaimed as the most skilled builders. Although U.S. authorities were initially unsure about the dome as a pavilion, it was an extraordinary success, attracting more attention than all other exhibits, including both Russian and Chinese exhibits. Locals climbed on the dome, and the King of Afghanistan even requested it as a gift, launching the geodesic dome on a glittering career as a trade-fair pavilion. The geodesic dome was felt to "dramatize American ingenuity". Fuller was the American inventor *par excellence* – the dome a powerful, lightweight, propaganda tool that "kept the Russian engineers busy sketching". Geodesic domes were soon seen in trade fairs in Poznan, Casablanca, Tunis, Salonika, Istanbul, Madras, Delhi, Mombay, Rangoon, Bangkok, Tokyo and Osaka, crammed full of seductive American consumer goods and labour-saving devices. The domes were the ingenious omni-triangulated wrapping for a "U.S. wonderland" of commodities.

The U.S. pavilion for the Moscow trade fair of 1959 was a 200-foot diameter gold-anodized aluminium geodesic dome. The dome contained a television demonstration by RCA, a computer by IBM and an Explorer VI satellite from NASA. The geodesic dome of the U.S. exhibit was the scene of the famous

127

Experimental plydome, University of
Michigan, 1954

Oberlin sphere (rhombic triacontahedral
grid), 1953

Interior of steel Union Tank Car dome, Baton Rouge, 1958, showing the central parts area with a second interior dome

Milan Triennale geodesic pavilion, 1957

"kitchen debate" between Nikita Kruschev and Richard Nixon over the relative benefits of U.S. capitalism and Russian communism. Reportedly, Kruschev said that "I would like to have R. Buckminster Fuller come to Russia and teach our engineers" after seeing the dome, a clear victory for American ingenuity. The U.S. exhibit also included film and slide projects by Ray and Charles Eames of "things too big to bring to Moscow", including dams, highways and bridges.

The Moscow dome was built by Kaiser Aluminum, one of the first companies to license Fuller's patent for the geodesic dome. When Don Richter, Fuller's student from the Chicago Institute of Design, went to work for Kaiser Aluminum in 1956, he had a model of the geodesic dome in his office. On seeing the model, Henry J. Kaiser expressed curiosity, and shortly afterwards he ordered a 145 foot dome as an auditorium for his Hawaiian Village in Honolulu. The dome, made of aluminium sheets that were braced on the outside, was erected and opened with a concert on the same day, and Kaiser subsequently developed many other domes as auditoria, exploiting their unusual acoustic qualities.

The largest geodesic dome project of this period was the enormous steel dome built by Union Tank Car Company in Baton Rouge, Louisiana. Union Tank Car required a plant where they could repair and repaint railway cars. Wrapping the cars around a central parts area appeared to be a practical solution, and a geodesic dome seemed like the best way to cover the large circular space. The welded-steel dome, completed in 1958, spanned 384 feet, making it by far the largest clear-span structure in the world. A smaller second dome, serving little practical function, surrounded the elevator shaft in the parts area. Fuller not-

Geoscope, School of Architecture,
Nottingham (England)

Fuller's "geoscope", a 21-foot diameter
geodesic sphere representing the Earth,
Cornell University, 1952

ed that the entire cathedral of Seville could fit comfortably inside the Baton Rouge dome, yet the completed structure weighed only as much as four of the more than one hundred stone columns that made up the structure in Seville. After a later visit to Seville, Fuller triumphantly scribed a dome on a postcard containing the cathedral. Union Tank Car built an identical dome in Wood River, Illinois.

If the Baton Rouge dome was the world's largest geodesic structure (as it remained until Donald Richter's 1982 415-foot dome-hangar built to house Howard Hughes' *Spruce Goose*), Fuller's most beautiful geodesic dome was undoubtedly the dome created for the U.S. Pavilion in the 1967 Expo at Montreal. The 250-foot diameter dome, constructed by Fuller and Sadao with Geometrics Inc. and Associated Architects, was a three-quarter sphere. Below the equator the horizontals were lesser circles, above the equator it was geodesic. A futuristic raised monorail brought visitors into the dome. Fuller originally wanted to have the dome house a World Game – a participatory simulation of global economics, and an animated version of his Geoscope. However, the organizers opposed the idea, and instead the US pavilion was dedicated to "Creative America" including an exhibition, *American Painting Now* with works by Andy Warhol, Roy Lichtenstein, and, most notably, a giant painting representing Fuller's icosahedral Dymaxion Air-Ocean Map by Jasper Johns, in addition to an Apollo spacecraft and various other items of 1960s Americana. The monorail gave the exhibit the atmosphere of a ride, a foretaste of Disney's Spaceship Earth at the Epcot Center

Union Tank Car Dome, Wood River, Illinois

Fuller's sketch on a postcard from Seville showing the cathedral fitting inside the Montreal Expo '67 dome

Fuller with dome models

(which Fuller also wanted to contain a World Game). The exhibition itself, as a representation of American culture divorced from consumerism was held in little esteem by visitors. The dome, on the other hand, was sensational, and outshone even Moshe Safdie's modular Habitat '67 and Frei Otto's tension structure over the West German Pavilion. The dome was sealed with a transparent skin of acrylic glass panels, and the amount of light allowed in could be controlled by moveable, triangular sunshades on the inside, that changed according to the position of the sun. A computer programme was supposed to guide the shading system, but unfortunately on the first day the operating cables twisted, leaving all the shades jammed in a random position. Years later, while conducting maintenance work on the dome in 1976, a careless welder ignited the acrylic skin, turning the dome into a giant geodesic fireball.

[44] Richard Guy Wilson, *The AIA Gold Medal*, McGraw Hill Book Company, New York, 1984, p. 210.
[45] See Alex Pang, "Dome Days: Buckminster Fuller in the Cold War", in Francis Spufford and Jenny Uglow, eds., *Cultural Babbage: Technology, Time and Invention*, Faber and Faber, London, 1997, pp. 167-192.
[46] *Tensegrity (1958)*, in Krausse and Lichtenstein, eds., *Your Private Sky Discourse*, cit., pp. 229-242.
[47] Pang, *Dome Days*, cit.

U.S. Marine Corps helilifting a 55-foot dome, 1954

WORLD AROUND AIR DISTRIBUTABLE
HIGH STANDARD OF LIVING PACKAGE

WITH SCIENCE DESIGNED PERFORMANCE—PER UNITS OF INVESTED
RESOURCE — SO HIGH THAT TOTAL WORLD RESOURCES MAY ADE-
QUATELY SERVE AND KEEP PACE WITH TOTAL WORLD PEOPLES
GROWTH. A MESSAGE OF TEAMED EFFECTIVENESS OF INDIVIDUAL
INITIATIVE AND ECONOMIC DESIGN RESPONSIBILITY THAT IS DEM-
ONSTRATING SPONTANEOUS COMPREHENSION.

CONFIDENTIAL: FOR PRIVATE INSPECTION ONLY

Air-deliverable housing, Fuller's lifelong dream, 1954

U.S. Marine Corps dome at National Air Show, Philadelphia, 1955

Geodesic dome aboard an aircraft carrier,
U.S.S. *Leyte*, 1957

U.S. Marine Corps helilifting a dome, 1957

U.S. Marine Corps, aluminium dome,
Quantico, Virginia, 1954

U.S. Marine Corps, magnesium dome,
Quantico, Virginia, 1954

U.S. Marine Corps, paper dome, Quantico,
Virginia, 1954

Artist's conception of an advanced air-base
with geodesic dome shelters in place. The
large aircraft hangars would have to be
airlifted in sections, 1954

The geodesic dome as a weapon: dome-
hangars being dropped into the battlefield,
1954

Radome in construction, Lincoln Lab, M.I.T.,
1955

Radome, Lincoln Laboratory, MIT, 1954

The Distant Early Warning (DEW) line

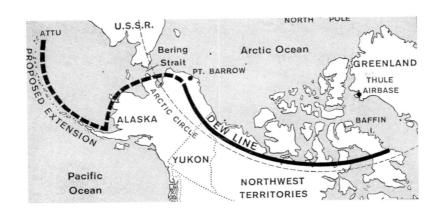

Radome, Long Island, New York, 1955

Radome in use on the Distant Early
Warning (DEW) line, 1954

U.S.A. pavilion, Kabul, Afghanistan, 1956

10-foot playdome of Matrix, Inc., supporting
11 men and a child, 1957

Circarama USA, pavilion for Small Industry
Fair, Sri Lanka, 1961

Geodesic pavilion, U.S. Information Agency,
1957

147

View of interior of Circarama dome,
Sri Lanka, 1961

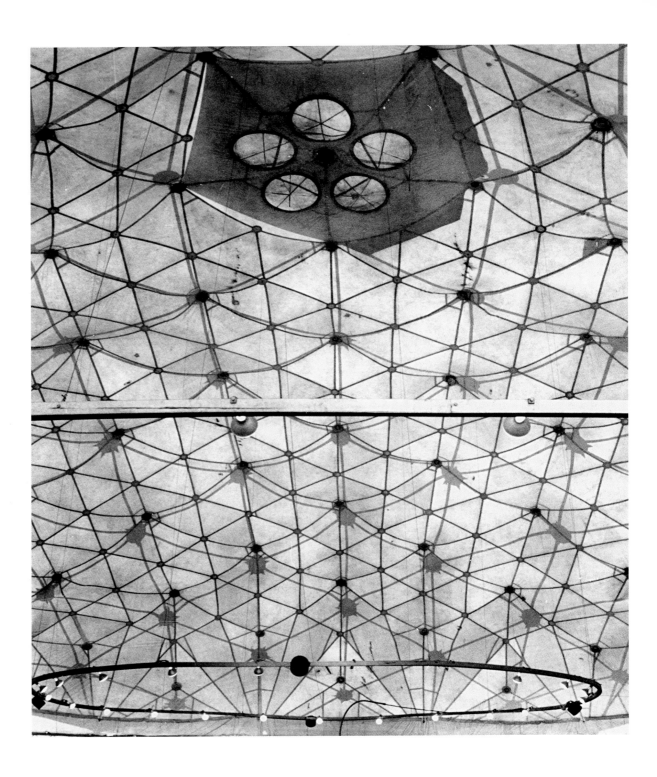

Radome being lifted into place on the top of
Mount Fuji, Japan

Minnesota dome, no. 3, August 1954

Geodesic dome, Botanical gardens,
Oaxtepec, Mexico, Synergetics, Inc., 1971

Geodesic dome, octet truss and tensegrity
mast displayed in MOMA gardens, New
York, 1959

Plydome, circa 1957

The Hollywood hills dome, from the
Los Angeles Times, July 1, 1962

Plydome construction, circa 1957

Geodesic dome home, Hollywood Hills
(1962). This was the dome that was
originally built in Montreal in 1950,
transferred to a steep hillside location

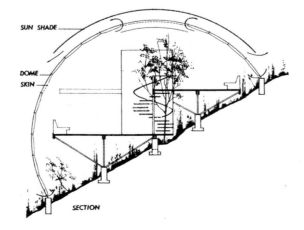

Cornell Pine Cone plydome, 1957

Interior view of Cornell Pine Cone Plydome, 1957

Wooden geodesic dome on Bear Island

Plydome, circa 1957

Involute-Hypercat Howard plydome

Fuller in his dome home, Carbondale,
Illinois

Fuller's dome home, Carbondale, Illinois

Tangent circles geodesic dome model,
Germany, 1962

Dome home made by Dura Dome, Colorado

Interior of the dome home made by Dura
Dome, Colorado

Geodesic dome and missile at the Mid-America Jubilee, St. Louis, 1956

Citizens State Bank, Oklahoma City, built by
Kaiser Aluminum

Interior of plydome made by Gene Godfrey,
Anaheim, California

250-foot diameter aluminium open frame
geodesic dome

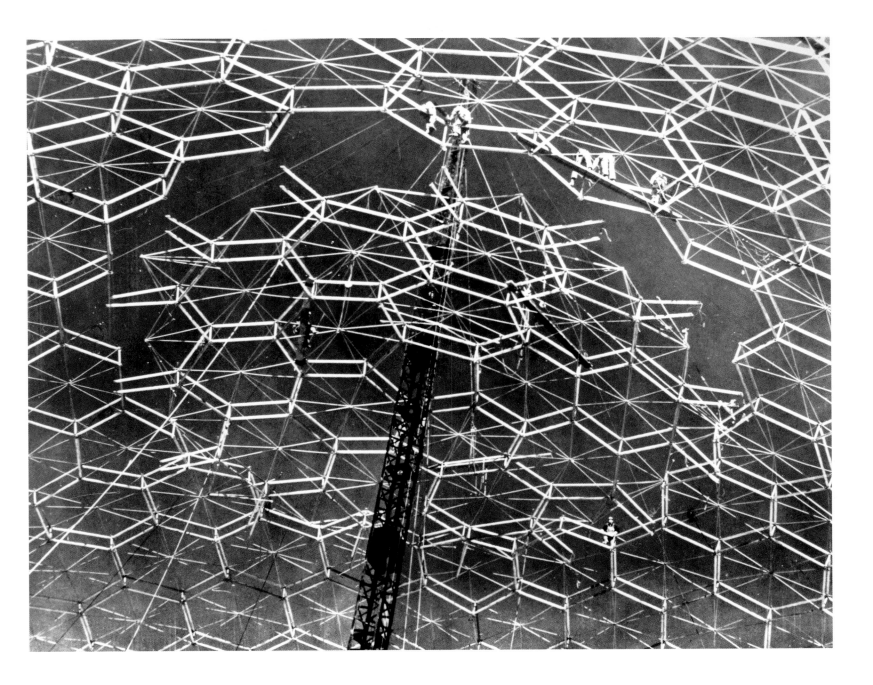

"American Painting Now" exhibition, inside
the Montreal Expo '67 geodesic dome

Cover of catalogue advertising "American Painting Now", the exhibition inside the Montreal Expo '67 dome

Model for the Montreal Expo '67 dome

Model of the Montreal Expo '67 dome, interior

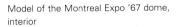

Model of the Montreal Expo '67 dome,
overhead view

Montreal Expo '67 dome, detail

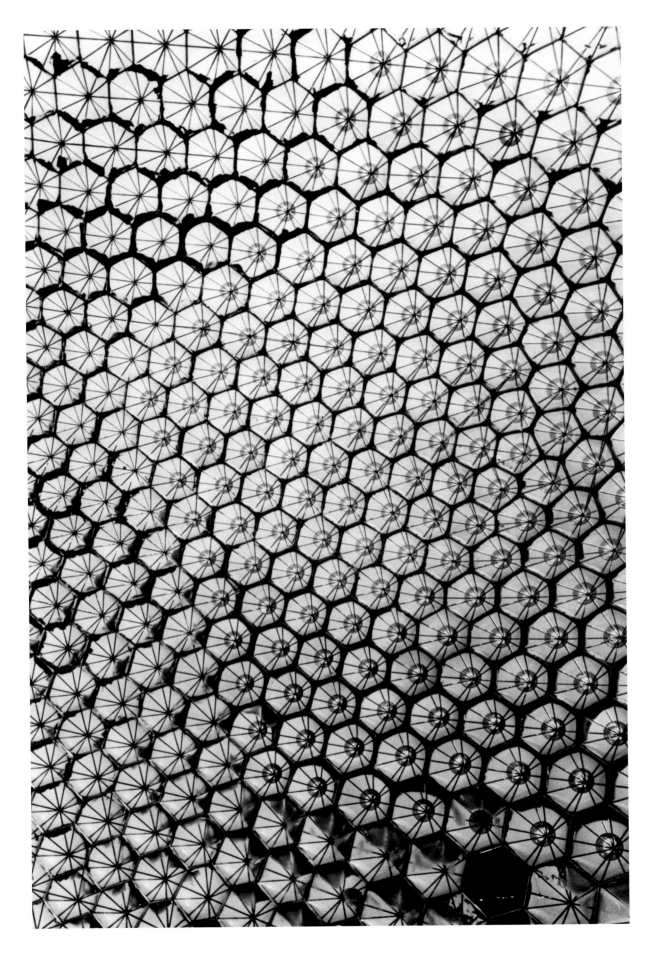

The Montreal Expo '67 dome in flames,
1976

Montreal Expo '67 dome

Hostesses at the U.S. exhibit in Fuller's
Montreal Expo '67 dome
Corbis

7. Featherlight Structures

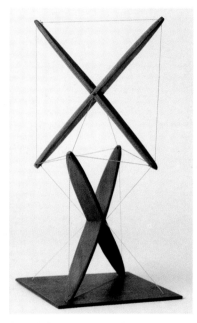

Kenneth Snelson, wooden X-piece, 1948.
This was the first example of a modular
tensegrity system.
Published with the kind permission of
Kenneth Snelson

As we have argued, Fuller's original goal of industrially produced air-deliverable shelter directed him on a lengthy investigation of ever lighter, tension-based structures. His 1929 Dymaxion House and 1946 Wichita House were based on the same structural principle as the bicycle wheel – compression elements (floors and mast) did not exert force on each other directly, but were linked via tension members (steel wires). Contrary to many people's impressions, a bicycle hangs from its spokes, which are incapable of bearing even a small compressional load. Tension based structures were already in use in many different contexts by civil engineers – with the suspension-bridges of the nineteenth century being the most celebrated example. Fuller was one of those (like the Vesnin brothers in Moscow) who were interested in creating architectural structures using tension. When Fuller arrived in Black Mountain College in the Summer of 1948, a young art student was assigned to help him prepare his models for the seminar. The student was Kenneth Snelson, and while he had originally come to Black Mountain College to have the chance to work with Josef Albers, he became more and more interested in Fuller's geometric investigations and took his seminar in Dymaxion geometry. During the Winter of 1948, Snelson experimented with modular mobile structures, somewhat similar to the mobiles of Alexander Calder. He replaced wire support elements with strings, and then experimented with using additional tension-strings to stabilize his structures. Eventually Snelson hit on a design where one wooden X-shaped piece was suspended, in apparent defiance of gravity, above another wooden X-shaped piece. The pieces did not touch each other, their points, suspended in space, constituted the vertices of an invisible octahedron. As Snelson recounts "Even though there was no longer any movement, the static structure was stranger than anything I could have imagined: rigid parts fixed in space one-to-another only by means of threads"[48].

Whereas other sculptors had experimented with structures involving combinations of tension members and compression members (struts), including Russian constructivist Karl Ioganson and Fuller's friend Isamu Noguchi, the true force of Snelson's discovery was to demonstrate that such structures could be extended in a modular way in all directions, to create masts and other large-scale structures.[49] Thus, without Snelson's serendipitous discovery, it was in no way imaginable that tension structures could constitute the building blocks for a new, lightweight architecture. In common with the move from a vertical mast to the "spherical mast" of the geodesic dome, Snelson demonstrated that tension structures could be extended in all directions to create networks of forces that counterbalanced each other.

As Fuller believed that the tetrahedron was nature's fundamental building block, immediately after seeing Snelson's plywood and monofilament X-piece he set about creating a tetrahedral version. Fuller described such structures as "tensegrity" structures – a word combining "tension" and "integrity". Tension

Fuller with a tensegrity mast and dome
model, circa 1950

Kenneth Snelson's "Dymaxion License"
from R Buckminster Fuller, allowing him to
practice Dymaxion Geometry, 1949
Published with the kind permission of
Kenneth Snelson

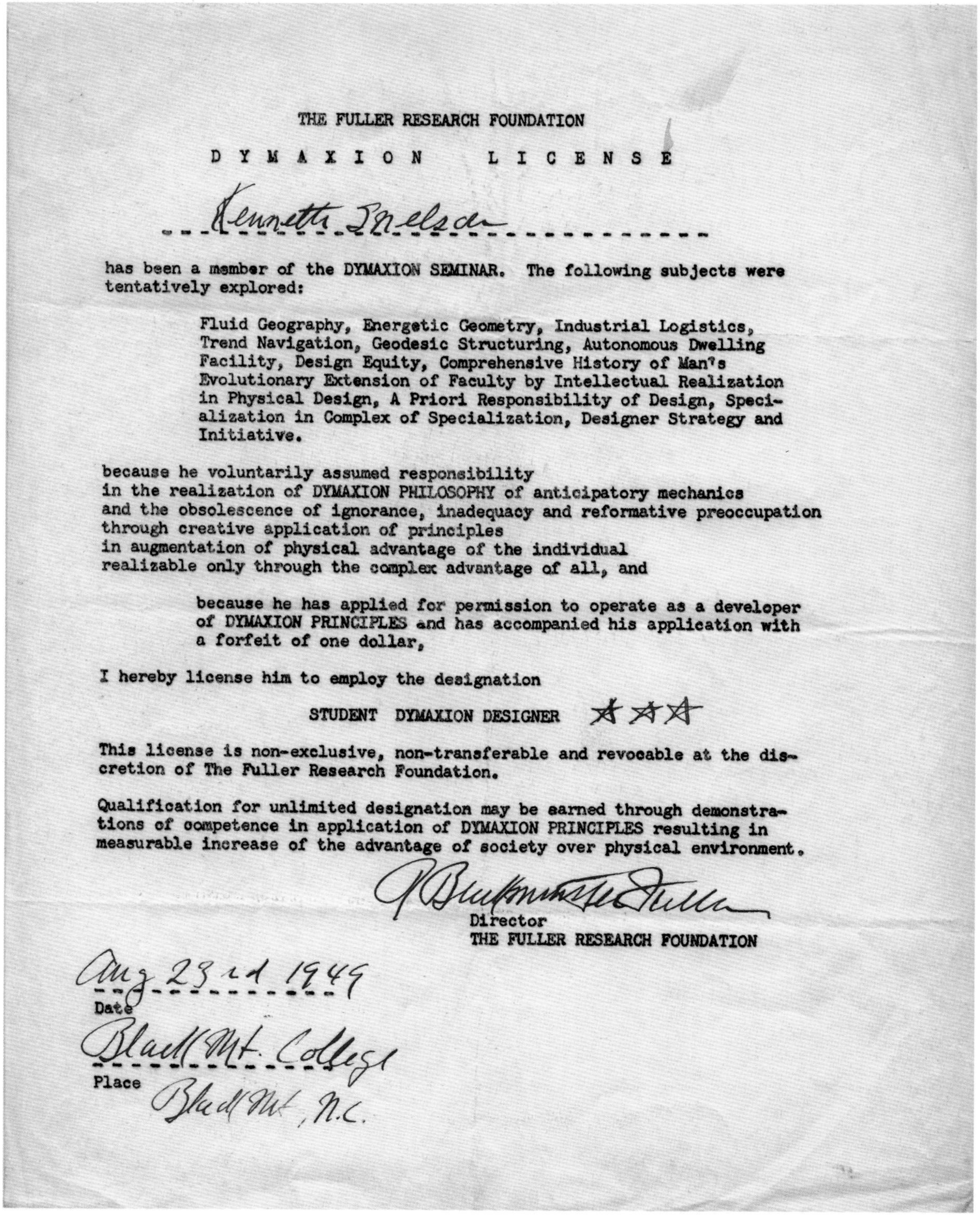

THE FULLER RESEARCH FOUNDATION

D Y M A X I O N   L I C E N S E

Kenneth Snelson

has been a member of the DYMAXION SEMINAR. The following subjects were
tentatively explored:

> Fluid Geography, Energetic Geometry, Industrial Logistics,
> Trend Navigation, Geodesic Structuring, Autonomous Dwelling
> Facility, Design Equity, Comprehensive History of Man's
> Evolutionary Extension of Faculty by Intellectual Realization
> in Physical Design, A Priori Responsibility of Design, Speci-
> alization in Complex of Specialization, Designer Strategy and
> Initiative.

because he voluntarily assumed responsibility
in the realization of DYMAXION PHILOSOPHY of anticipatory mechanics
and the obsolescence of ignorance, inadequacy and reformative preoccupation
through creative application of principles
in augmentation of physical advantage of the individual
realizable only through the complex advantage of all, and

> because he has applied for permission to operate as a developer
> of DYMAXION PRINCIPLES and has accompanied his application with
> a forfeit of one dollar,

I hereby license him to employ the designation

STUDENT DYMAXION DESIGNER

This license is non-exclusive, non-transferable and revocable at the dis-
cretion of The Fuller Research Foundation.

Qualification for unlimited designation may be earned through demonstrations of competence in application of DYMAXION PRINCIPLES resulting in
measurable increase of the advantage of society over physical environment.

Director
THE FULLER RESEARCH FOUNDATION

Aug 23rd 1949
Date

Black Mt. College
Place *Black Mt, N.C.*

First kinetic model demonstrating the
Jitterbug Transformation, 1948, preserved
in Stanford University Libraries.
Photograph: Sean Quimby

and integrity were also to play their roles in the long-standing dispute between Fuller and Snelson, later
to produce an extraordinary profusion of sculptures exploring the principle, over who had really "discovered" tensegrity. Fuller considered Snelson as a catalyst, Snelson was understandably irked when Fuller did
not acknowledge his contribution and patented tensegrity structures, including tetrahedral masts and
tensegrity spheres, in 1962, but we have seen that this was entirely in keeping with Fuller's highly rationalized approach to intellectual property. Fuller implied that Snelson was only interested in tensegrity as
a means for producing works of art, while he was interested in Snelson's work as a special case demonstration of a generalized principle. On the difference in approach between the artist and the comprehensive designer, Fuller wrote "I have shunned the daily recurrent opportunities to exploit Energetic-Synergetic
Geometry either as toys or *objets d'art*".

He insisted that Snelson, the artist, was the unwitting vehicle of a principle that Fuller had sought
for many years: "No one else in the world but I could have seen the significance I saw in what you showed
me"[50]. In representing Snelson as an artist uninterested in general principles, Fuller has been proved wrong
– Snelson's work has included a tensegrity model for the atom, and has also been the basis for Donald Ingber's investigations into the structure of the cell. As Ingber remarks, "tensegrity structures are mechanically stable not because of the strength of the individual members but because of the way the entire
structure distributes and balances mechanical stresses". The main difference between a tensegrity struc-

179

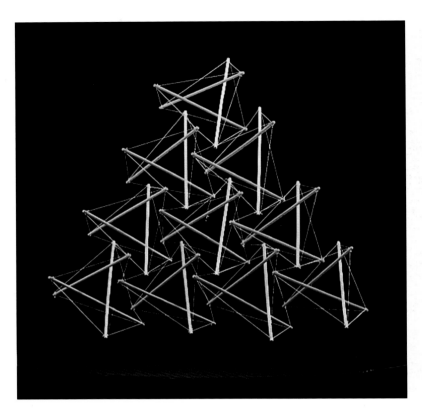

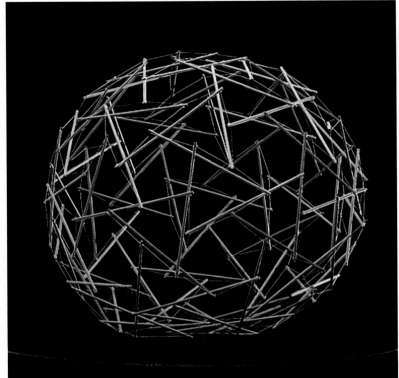

ture and, for example, a geodesic dome is that while all of the metal struts in a geodesic dome are capable of bearing both compression and tension, some of the members in a tensegrity structure are only capable of bearing tension (Snelson's monofilament fishing line, for example). To confuse the issue, some have called the dome a tensegrity structure, to the detriment of the precise meaning of the word – Fuller regarded the dome, somewhat dubiously, as a "limiting case" of tensegrity, at least for the purpose of the priority dispute.

If tension is increased on one member of a tensegrity structure, then it is increased on all members simultaneously. If you suspend a fairly slack tensegrity sphere from the ceiling, for example, it will expand in all directions to make a taut spherical shape. Ingber used six wooden dowels and some elastic string to make a simple tensegrity model of the biological cell, which, along with several subsequent models, predicted phenomena not predicted by other available models. As the phenomenon of tensegrity provided Ingber with a helpful model of the distribution of physical forces in the cell, so familiarity with the geodesic dome allowed Harold W. Kroto to develop a model of the Carbon 60 molecule as a truncated icosahedron or soccer-ball shape, a discovery that earned Kroto, Smalley and Curl the Nobel prize in 1996. In honour of Fuller's Expo '67 dome the molecule was christened *Buckminsterfullerene*, to be colloquially known as the "Buckyball".

Fuller's demonstrations of geometrical principles through built structures, frequently achieved by harnessing (and occasionally exploiting) some of the most brilliant and inventive young minds available, provided structural models and lessons that could be imported into many different fields of investigation. When he was told by Arthur Loeb that according to Arthur Coxeter, the deadliest viruses were those that most closely approximated geodesic domes, Fuller retorted that he was unsurprised because they would be the most stable. His intuitive, hands-on, non-deductive approach, while it made his writings indigestible

Triangular tensegrity model, preserved in
Stanford University Libraries.
Photograph: Stanford Visual Art Services

Spherical tensegrity model, preserved in
Stanford University Libraries.
Photograph: Stanford Visual Art Services

Building a 40-foot tensegrity hemisphere,
Minneapolis, Minnesota, 1953

to most scientists, had enormous advantages for "rapid prototyping" of structures, the development of tangible models unhindered by pedantic proofs.

Inspired by Snelson's discovery, which Snelson used as the point of departure for his remarkable tensegrity sculptures, Fuller and his students constructed numerous tensegrity polyhedra and, in 1951, a large tensegrity mast that was later exhibited at the Museum of Modern Art in New York. The fact that a tensegrity icosahedron could be made implied that a tensegrity version of the geodesic dome should also be possible, as almost all domes are developed from the spherical icosahedron. In 1953, Fuller developed a 90-strut tensegrity sphere at Princeton University. Fuller was convinced that tensegrity was Nature's great structural secret, perhaps one of the reasons that he invested so much in defending his priority on this issue. "Nothing in Universe touches anything else", he exclaimed. Kepler had revealed that the solar system was a tension-system – a series of planetary rims around a single hub. Now Fuller could intuit that the "illusion" of solid matter was achieved through minute tensegrity structures. Tensegrity is the most economic way of producing large stable structures with the lightest component elements. Atoms, molecules, viruses, cells and planetary systems were all, for Fuller, different instantiations of the same general principle. Fuller even suggested a dizzying fractal vision of tensegrity, whereby the compression struts making up a tensegrity sphere were revealed to be tensegrity masts, whose own struts were in turn revealed under the microscope to be tensegrities, reminiscent of Augustus de Morgan's famous couplet "Great fleas have little fleas upon their backs to bite 'em, And little fleas have lesser fleas, and so ad infinitum"[51]. All compression members could thus be regarded as the macroscopic manifestation of a tensegrity system. If the study of the properties of the cuboctahedron had revealed to Fuller Nature's own coordinate system, tensegrity appeared to reveal her building blocks.

Regardless of the grand cosmic implications of tensegrity, one might wonder about the implica-

90-rod tensegrity sphere, Princeton
University, 1953

Tensegrity hemisphere (note that it is
suspended from above), Minneapolis,
Minnesota, 1953

Sketch for a 2-mile diameter dome covering lower Manhattan

Cloud Nine floating geodesic cities: "As geodesic spheres get larger than one-half mile in diameter they become floatable cloud structures… Such sky-floating geodesic spheres may be designed to float at preferred altitudes of thousands of feet. The weight of human beings added to such prefabricated "cloud nines" would be relatively negligible. Many thousands of passengers could be housed aboard one-mile diameter and larger cloud structures. The passengers could come and go from cloud to cloud, or cloud to ground, as the clouds float around the earth or are anchored to mountain tops".
R. Buckminster Fuller

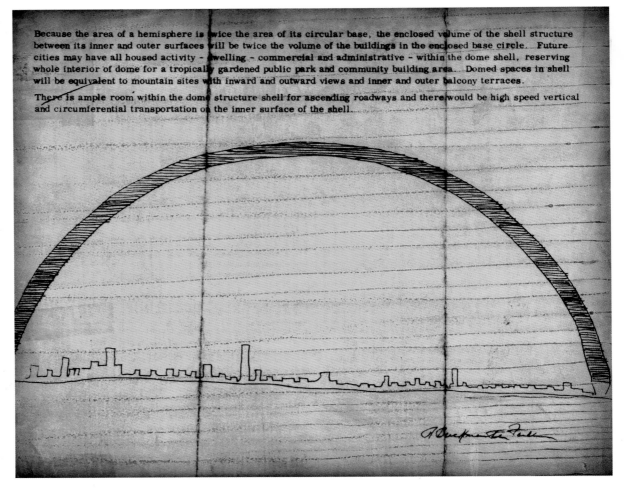

Because the area of a hemisphere is twice the area of its circular base, the enclosed volume of the shell structure between its inner and outer surfaces will be twice the volume of the buildings in the enclosed base circle. Future cities may have all housed activity - dwelling - commercial and administrative - within the dome shell, reserving whole interior of dome for a tropically gardened public park and community building area. Domed spaces in shell will be equivalent to mountain sites with inward and outward views and inner and outer balcony terraces.

There is ample room within the dome structure shell for ascending roadways and there would be high speed vertical and circumferential transportation on the inner surface of the shell.

tions of the discovery for built structures. Tensegrity spheres could be made using minimal material investment to produce a large, extremely light structure that was resistant to deformation. Even in 1958, Fuller was suggesting that tensegrity structures could be shot to the Moon, and also used for satellites. Fuller saw in tensegrity structures the potential to overcome some of the size constraints that even geodesic domes had to face – constraints on scaling built structures that had been indicated by Galileo Galilei in his *Two New Sciences* of 1638.

Fuller argued that the very light weight of tensegrity spheres meant that there was no practical limit on their size. He considered a tensegrity sphere of several miles in diameter surrounded by transparent polyethylene skin. As the sun heated the air inside the sphere, it would become several degrees warmer than the air outside, causing it to rise above the ground, given the negligible weight of the structure with respect to the air. Fuller imagined floating *Cloud Nine Cities* anchored to mountaintops, with populations of several thousand people (see front cover). Alternatively, the Cloud Nine Cities could be allowed to drift at a preferred altitude, allowing human beings to migrate like birds. The weight of the people inside the structure would be small compared to the upthrust produced by the heated air. Entering and leaving Cloud Nine Cities would be more complicated, although for a sufficient size Fuller argued that a skin would not even be necessary. Fuller's speculations on the practical applications of tensegrity structures have proved over-optimistic.

Producing a tensegrity dome for terrestrial use proved somewhat more challenging than build-

ing tensegrity spheres and polyhedra. In 1953, Fuller gave this task to his students at the University of Min-nesota, and they produced a tensegrity hemisphere made from cigar-shaped polyester-fibreglass rods. This dome, modelled directly on a 270-strut tensegrity sphere was, however, suspended from above to prevent collapse, as close inspection of the photographs reveals. Fuller did incorporate tensegrity elements into a number of geodesic domes built after this time – for example, the Montreal Expo '67 dome made use of "star tensegrity", or tensegrity octahedra on each facet, providing additional strength through the creation of tensegrity octet truss elements. Fuller also designed a non-geodesic structure called an "aspension" dome which used lesser- circle arrangements of tensegrity structures, patented in 1964, but lacking the advan-tageous structural properties of geodesics. The synergetic structural properties of tensegrity spheres were not generally shared by tensegrity hemispheres, one reason why floating and space-bound structures were particularly appropriate applications for tensegrity.

[48] Kenneth Snelson, "Snelson on the Tensegrity Invention", *International Journal of Space Structures*, vol. 11, nos. 1 and 2, 1996, pp. 43-48.
[49] On Ioganson see Maria Gough, "In the labo-ratory of Constructivism: Karl Ioganson's Cold Structures", *October*, no. 84, Spring 1996, pp. 91-117.

[50] E.J. Applewhite, "R. Buckminster Fuller on pri-ority of tensegrity: Excerpts from Fuller's Let-ter to Snelson", *International Journal of Space Structures*, vol. 11, nos. 1 and 2, 1996, pp. 43-48.
[51] Augustus de Morgan, *A Budget of Paradoxes*, p. 377.

8. Eden?

Fuller's reflections on floating tensegrity spheres led him to hypothesize that even in a landlocked geodesic dome, at very large scales the upthrust of heated air on the skin would tend to counterbalance the weight of the structure. This insight made him optimistic for the possibility of ever-larger geodesic structures making use of tensegrity elements. In an interview with *Playboy* magazine in 1968, Fuller audaciously suggested enclosing a large section of Lower Manhattan in a two-mile diameter geodesic dome. According to Fuller's calculations, such a dome would reduce energy losses (from air-conditioning in Summer through the "chilling effect" and heating in Winter) to 1/85 of their present levels, and also remove the need for snow removal, creating a semi-tropical "greenhouse" climate inside the dome. The dome would, Fuller argued, be almost invisible to people underneath it. Rainwater would be channelled down the sides of the dome and collected in reservoirs. Clearly, human and industrial air-pollution beneath the dome would need to be eradicated. Fuller's Manhattan dome is a new version of the medieval walled city (another version had two large domes, one of which would have covered the World Trade Center).

Fuller's 4D vision of 1928 had been a vision of human dispersal – cities were filthy, polluted and unsuitable spaces for bringing up children, so 4D homes would be airlifted to secluded, healthy places, with Fuller's Bear Island being the paradigm for a redistribution of humankind. Nonetheless, in the 1960s and 1970s, Fuller returned to the problem of the city. In 1966 Fuller developed a project for a two-mile-high tetrahedral tower with Japanese billionaire Matsaturo Shoriki, but the project had to be abandoned due to problems including the effects of 300 mile-an-hour winds on the tower, the dangers of large ice shards falling from the higher structures, and the challenges of providing oxygen to visitors using the observation deck at the top of the tower. The cost of the project, which bears a structural and functional resemblance to Alexander Graham Bell's more modest tetrahedral observation tower of 1907, was estimated at over 1,5 billion dollars in 1966, placing it beyond the reach of even Shoriki's ample resources.

Unperturbed, Shoriki commissioned Fuller to conduct research for the design of a new kind of city to house a million people. Fuller developed a design for a tetrahedral city, which was intended to float in Tokyo Bay. The reason for the tetrahedral shape was that a spherical surface provides the greatest volume for the least surface area, as every soap bubble demonstrates, but a tetrahedron is the most stable structure that has the greatest surface area. As Fuller envisaged the inhabitants occupying the surface of the city, so everyone would have a room with a view, a tetrahedral shape was the most efficient solution, while ensuring the maximum stability of the whole structure. Lewis Mumford, once considered by Scribner as a possible ghostwriter for Fuller's description of the Dymaxion House, condemned Fuller's tetrahedral city in his *Pentagon of Power* as a new kind of pyramid, "big enough to entomb a whole city". He

Fuller in front of a 26-foot Fly's Eye dome

Fuller's projected dome over lower
Manhattan, photomontage, 1960

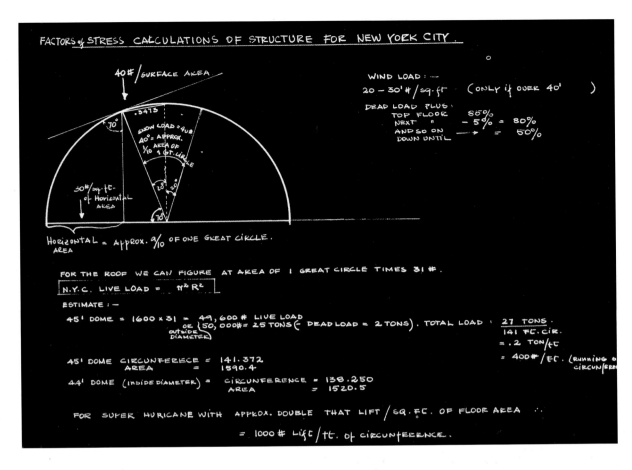

attacked Fuller's tetrahedral vision as a product of "autocratic technocracy", a throwback to the Pharaonic age and a reflection of the "impulse to suppress human variety and autonomy, and to make every need and impulse conform to the system of collective control imposed by the autocratic designer"[52]. Mumford's critique does raise important questions: was Fuller's approach to design an affront to the dignity of the individual human being? When his daughter asked him "What is a man?" Fuller replied "a self-balancing, 28-jointed adapter-base biped, an electro-chemical reduction plant, integral with the segregated stowages of special energy extracts in storage batteries, for subsequent actuation of thousands of hydraulic and pneumatic pumps, with motors attached; 62,000 miles of capillaries, millions of warning-signal, railroad, and conveyor systems; crushers and cranes [...] and a universally distributed telephone system needing no service for 70 years if well managed; the whole, extraordinarily complex mechanism guided with exquisite precision from a turret in which are located telescopic and microscopic self-registering and recording range finders"[53].

Fuller was a technophile, certainly. His vision was an upbeat, modernist faith in the dramatic improvement of people's lives made possible by the economies brought about by mass-production, materials research and the latest communications technology. But, Pharaonic patronage aside, Fuller was never really more than a lukewarm advocate of a "Megalopolis" city of the future. Invited to participate in Constantin Doxiadis's Delos Symposium on Ekistics or the "science of human settlements", Fuller responded that he did not really believe in the city as a unit of analysis, and, with the exception of a small number of projects such as the domed "Old Man River city" proposed for East St. Louis, Illinois, Fuller did not devote much of his long career to city design.

Fuller's career began and ended with the problem of the home. But what was it actually like to inhabit one of Fuller's structures? In the late 1960s and early 1970s, many hippie communities carried out experiments in communal living. Stewart Brand's *Whole Earth Catalog*, published in 1968 and dedicated to R. Buckminster Fuller ("The insights of Buckminster Fuller are what initiated this catalog"), inspired countless drop-outs to build domes and go back to the land. Lloyd Kahn produced *Domebook* I and II in the early 1970s providing more tips on how to construct domes, and graphic reports from the front lines. The Red Rockers, one commune in Colorado, exclaimed that "there's no point in building revolutionary structures to shelter reactionary life-styles". Rejecting any "oppressive division of labour", all the Red Rockers were domebuilders, making "domes and Revolution together"[54]. Perhaps the most notorious of the communes was Drop City in Colorado, an obligatory point of passage for young freaks and hippies on the way West to the Haight Ashbury, immortalized in a psychedelic first-person account by "Peter Rabbit". The goal of Drop City was "constant orgasm". The inhabitants made domes and "zomes" by hacking up car-tops. "Peter Rabbit" outlined the universal benefits of geodesic constructions in euphoric terms : "Domes use materials in the most reasonable, efficient way. Bucky Fuller gave Drop City the 1966 Dymaxion Award for poetically economic structural accomplishments. Soon domed cities will spread across the world, anywhere land is cheap – on the deserts, in the swamps, on mountains, tundras, ice caps. The tribes are moving, building completely free and open way-stations, each a warm and beautiful conscious environment. We are winning".

In his later study *How Buildings Learn*, one-time dome-evangelist Stewart Brand cast a cold eye on the geodesic dome as a living space with the benefit of hindsight: "As a major propagandist for Fuller domes in my Whole Earth Catalogs, I can report with mixed chagrin and glee that they were a massive, total failure. Count the ways [...] Domes leaked, always. The angles between the facets could never be sealed successfully. If you gave up and tried to shingle the whole damn thing – dangerous process, ugly result – the nearly horizontal shingles on top still took in water. The inside was basically one big room, impossible to subdivide, with too much space wasted up high. The shape made it a whispering gallery that broad-

Model of Tetrahedron City designed for
Tokyo bay, now in Lyndon B. Johnson
Library, Austin, Texas, 1967

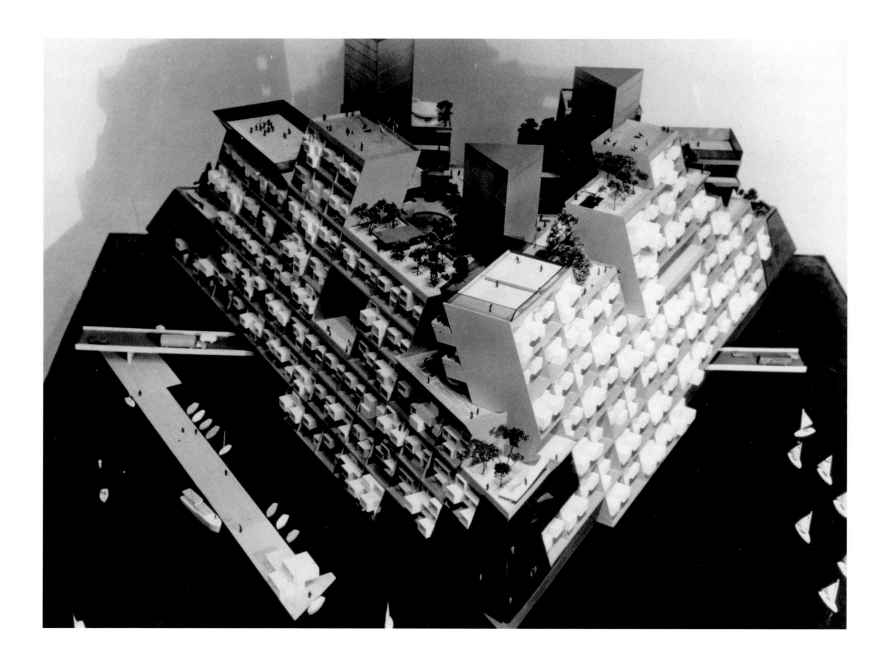

Model of Tetrahedron City designed for
Tokyo bay, now in Lyndon B. Johnson
Library, Austin, Texas, 1967

cast private sounds to everyone in the dome. Construction was a nightmare because everything was non-standard – contractors who have worked on domes all swear that they'll never do another. Even the vaunted advantage of saving on materials with a dome didn't work out, because cutting triangles and pentagons from rectangular sheets of plywood left enormous waste […] When my generation outgrew the domes, we simply left them empty, like hatchlings leaving their eggshells"[55].

As another one-time apostle of the dome, *Domebook* editor Lloyd Kahn put it: "What's good about 90-degree walls: they don't catch dust, rain doesn't sit on them, easy to add to; gravity, not tension, holds them in place. It's easy to build in counters, shelves, arrange furniture, bathtubs, beds. We are 90 degrees to the earth".

As an advocate of industrialization, Fuller may appear an unlikely hero for the 1960s counter-culture in any case, and one can imagine that he looked askance on the handmade geometrical monstrosities of Drop City, a striking contrast to the neat array of geodesic radomes along the DEW line, rendered practically obsolete as soon as they were installed by the launch of Sputnik and the advent of the ICBM.

The problem of the air-deliverable single family home was one that Fuller returned to again and again in the course of his career. The *Skybreak Dome* of 1949 was an autonomous dwelling, a climate-controlling skin that contained fruit trees in addition to the furniture and equipment contained in the Standard of Living Package developed by Fuller's students in Chicago. The Climatron in St. Louis Missouri, developed under license by local architects, was a true domed garden, filled with tropical palms and arrow-poison frogs. The Pillowdomes created by Jay Baldwin with the New Alchemy Institute from 1969-1977 were Garden of Eden domes skinned with triangular vinyl pillows, later the vinyl was replaced with Tefzel, a plastic that does not deteriorate in sunlight, inflated with argon gas. In addition to being a living space for humans, Pillowdomes supported the cultivation of fish and vegetables.

Fuller set out in 1928 with the problem of defining the single family home. Like Le Corbusier, he immediately saw that industrial manufacture could be as revolutionary for the single-family home as it had been for the automobile. For Fuller, the home could be addressed as a problem of providing shelter and intellectual and material autonomy. It was an "environment control", or "environment valve". Fuller's use of the terms "environment" and "environmental design" are, it must be conceded, very different from those later adopted by the environmentalist movement. Fuller conceived the home as a membrane surrounding a space, and defining an inhabitable microclimate. His geodesic domes, Dymaxion Dwelling Units and Wichita House were environment controls, in the same way that a refrigerator is an environment control. Fuller, in his banker's suit and tie, did not consider the "environment" as something to be preserved or respected – he regarded it as something to be controlled.

Nonetheless, his ideas about domestic autonomy and independence from "grids" – sewage, electricity, schools, and water – encouraged him to develop solutions to the problem of the home that incorporated recycling of waste, maximum use of solar and wind energy and other "environmentally friendly" strategies, to use a term that would have been alien to Fuller. For Fuller, these strategies were not directed by a moral imperative – they were simply dictated by sound economics and a systems approach to the problem. If Fuller was an ecologist, his was an out-and-out capitalist, anti-regulatory, and 100% American version of ecology, something that the Red Rockers appear to have misunderstood. Sulphur Dioxide escaping from a factory chimney was not, in Fuller's view, morally reprehensible pollution – it was simply the eco-

Project of city megastructure designed for
Toronto, 1969

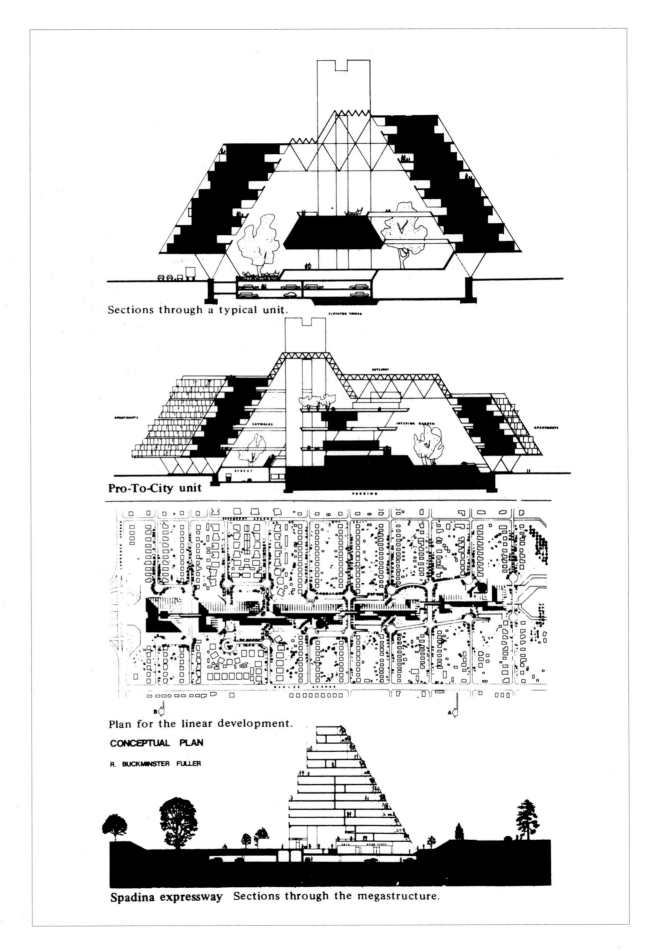

Sections through a typical unit.

Pro-To-City unit

Plan for the linear development.

CONCEPTUAL PLAN

R. BUCKMINSTER FULLER

Spadina expressway Sections through the megastructure.

Shaw botanic gardens, St. Louis, Missouri,
1960

Yomiuri "Star" Inagamachi Golf Club Field House, 1961-3

nomically reprehensible waste of perfectly good chemicals that could be used to make other useful products. As Nature was Fuller's ultimate instructor in economical design, from bubbles to birds, from viruses to radiolaria, his approach was in some sense a precursor to today's ecological design. As an inveterate steak-eater and erstwhile meat-packer, Fuller was not terribly interested in "caring for nature", he was much more interested in looking to nature for highly developed examples of comprehensive design strategies.

Fuller's ideal autonomous living space was intended as a womb-like microcosm of the planet earth, itself an autonomous dwelling machine with a gaseous envelope, as implied by his famous phrase "Space-ship Earth". Fuller's 1970s *Fly's Eye Dome* (based on a 1965 patent) which would have looked good on the set of *Barbarella*, was also intended as an autonomous living space. Even in 1979, Fuller was trying to get the students of the Art Center College of Design in Pasadena to implement a fog-gun shower for the Fly's Eye, with a view to finally completing his 1928 project.

In spite of the many difficulties experienced by those who attempted to inhabit Fuller's structures his lifelong goal of intellectual and practical autonomy in a redefined home remains a seductive possibility. His approach to autonomous living, and his far-reaching philosophy of the home, divested of any specific architectural incarnation, is perhaps his most important legacy, and its influence can be seen in contemporary projects from Lord Norman Foster's Reichstag in Berlin to Nicholas Grimshaw's Eden project in Cornwall, from the sustainable design initiatives of William McDonough and Michael Braungart to author Paul Hawken's *Natural Capitalism* and John Todd's *Living Machines*, deploying biological systems to purify water and produce useful products from "waste".

Such strategies, representing just one strand in contemporary ecological thinking, are very dif-

Yomiuri "Star" Inagamachi Golf Club Field
House, 1961-3

Botanical gardens, Oaxtepec, Mexico,
Geodesic dome by Synergetics, Inc., 1971

Interior of geodesic dome greenhouse,
Shaw botanic gardens, St. Louis, Missouri,
1960

Old Man River, an umbrellaed town concept for East St. Louis, 1973

ferent from the regulatory approach that has characterized the "eco-efficiency" strategy in dealing with industrial pollution. They have their roots in the same economic paradigm that motivates the corporations, being presented as more efficient ways to make a profit in the long term through a reexamination of the processes of industrial production. It remains to be seen, at this early stage, whether their adoption by the most polluting multi-national corporations will go beyond a corporate public relations exercise and really become a new industrial paradigm.

R. Buckminster Fuller, while certainly an iconoclast, was no anarchist. He idolized Henry Ford as the greatest artist of the twentieth century, and boasted that his first major client was "Mr. Industry himself". He believed that the military could be a crucial development ground for new technology, and similarly he believed that large, multi-national corporations could be a positive force in the world, providing they adopted a comprehensive approach to design rather than focusing on short-term selfish interests.

Fuller's buildings and philosophical principles remain as elusive and tantalizing as flying seed-pods, light, self-sufficient structures designed for mobile, independent thinkers.

[52] Lewis Mumford, *The Pentagon of Power*, in *The Myth of the Machine*, vol. 2, Harcourt, Brace & World New York, 1967-70.
[53] Fuller, *Nine Chains to the Moon* (1938), republished in Krausse and Lichtenstein, eds.,

Your Private Sky Discourse, cit., p. 106.
[54] Cited in Pang, *Dome Days*, cit., p. 167.
[55] Stewart Brand, *How Buildings Learn: what Happens after they're Built*, Viking, New York, NY, 1994, pp. 59-61.

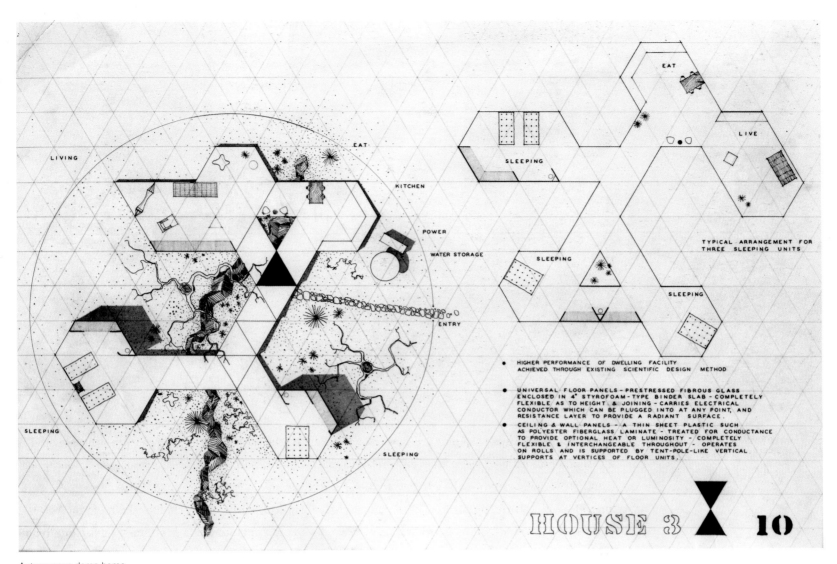

LIVING

EAT

KITCHEN

POWER

WATER STORAGE

ENTRY

SLEEPING

SLEEPING

EAT

SLEEPING

LIVE

TYPICAL ARRANGEMENT FOR
THREE SLEEPING UNITS

SLEEPING

SLEEPING

• HIGHER PERFORMANCE OF DWELLING FACILITY
ACHIEVED THROUGH EXISTING SCIENTIFIC DESIGN METHOD

• UNIVERSAL FLOOR PANELS - PRESTRESSED FIBROUS GLASS
ENCLOSED IN 4" STYROFOAM-TYPE BINDER SLAB - COMPLETELY
FLEXIBLE AS TO HEIGHT & JOINING - CARRIES ELECTRICAL
CONDUCTOR WHICH CAN BE PLUGGED INTO AT ANY POINT, AND
RESISTANCE LAYER TO PROVIDE A RADIANT SURFACE.

• CEILING & WALL PANELS - A THIN SHEET PLASTIC SUCH
AS POLYESTER FIBERGLASS LAMINATE - TREATED FOR CONDUCTANCE
TO PROVIDE OPTIONAL HEAT OR LUMINOSITY - COMPLETELY
FLEXIBLE & INTERCHANGEABLE THROUGHOUT - OPERATES
ON ROLLS AND IS SUPPORTED BY TENT-POLE-LIKE VERTICAL
SUPPORTS AT VERTICES OF FLOOR UNITS.

HOUSE 3 ▼▲ 10

Autonomous dome home,
designed by MIT students, circa 1952

8. EDEN?

Domes and Zomes made from car-tops, Drop City, Colorado, circa 1966

Fly's Eye dome, interior

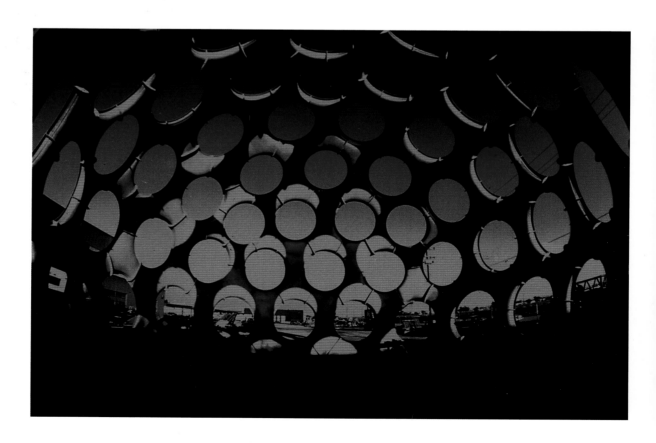

Selected Bibliography

Applewhite 1977
Applewhite, E.J., *Cosmic Fishing. An Account of Writing Synergetics with Buckminster Fuller*, Macmillan, New York, 1977.

Applewhite 1986
Applewhite, E.J. ed., *Synergetics Dictionary: The Mind of R. Buckminster Fuller*, 4 vols., Garland, New York, 1986.

Baldwin 1996
Baldwin, Jay, *Bucky Works: Buckminster Fuller's Ideas for Today*, Wiley, New York, 1996.

Edmondson 1987
Edmondson, Amy C., *A Fuller Explanation: The Synergetic Geometry of R. Buckminster Fuller*, Birkhauser Verlag (Design Science Collection), Boston, 1987.

Gabriel c 1997
Gabriel, J. François, ed., *Beyond the Cube: The Architecture of Space Frames and Polyhedra*, John Wiley, New York, c1997.

Hatch 1974
Hatch, Alden, *Buckminster Fuller: At Home in the Universe*, Crown Publishers, New York, 1974.

Jandl 1991
Jandl, H. Ward, *Yesterday's Houses of Tomorrow: Innovative American Homes 1850 to 1950*, The Preservation Press, Washington D.C., 1991.

Kenner 1973
Kenner, Hugh, *Bucky: A Guided Tour of Buckminster Fuller*, William Morrow, New York, 1973.

Kenner 1976
Kenner, Hugh, *Geodesic Math and How to Use It*, University of California Press, Berkeley, 1976, reprint 2003.

Krausse and Lichtenstein 1999
Krausse, Joachim and Claude Lichtenstein, eds., *Your Private Sky: R. Buckminster Fuller The Art of Design Science*, Lars Müller, Zürich, 1999.

Krausse and Lichtenstein 2001
Krausse, Joachim and Claude Lichtenstein, eds., *Your Private Sky: Discourse*, Lars Müller, Zürich, 2001.

Lalvani 1996
Lalvani, Haresh ed., "Origins of Tensegrity : Views of Emmerich, Fuller and Snelson" in *International Journal of Space Structures* , vol. 11, 1996, nos. 1 and 2, pp. 27-55.

Loeb 1976
Loeb, Arthur, *Space Structures: Their Harmony and Counterpoint*, Pearson Addison Wesley, London, 1976.

Marks 1973
Marks, Robert ed., *The Dymaxion World of Buckminster Fuller*, Doubleday, New York, 1973.

Pang 1997
Pang, Alex, "Dome Days: Buckminster Fuller in the Cold War", in *Cultural Babbage: Technology, Time and Invention*, Francis Spufford and Jenny Uglow, eds., Faber and Faber, London, 1997, pp. 167-192.

Snyder 1980
Snyder, Robert, *Buckminster Fuller: An Autographical Monologue Scenario*, St. Martin's Press, New York, 1980.

Ward 1984
Ward, James, *The Artifacts of R. Buckminster Fuller, A Comprehensive Collection of his Designs and Drawings*, 4 vols., Garland Publishing, New York, 1984.

Zung 2001
Zung, Thomas, ed., *Buckminster Fuller: Anthology for the New Millennium*, St. Martin's Press, New York, 2001.

Fuller's Writings
4D Timelock, Lama Foundation, Corrales, N.M: 1970 (first published privately in 1928).
Nine Chains to the Moon, Philadelphia, 1938, reprint Carbondale, Ill., 1963.
Education Automation, Carbondale, Ill., 1962.
Untitled Epic Poem on the History of Industrialization, New York, 1962.
Ideas and Integrities. A Spontaneous Autobiographical Disclosure, edited by Robert Marks, Englewood Cliffs, NJ, 1963.
No More Secondhand God and other Writings, Carbondale, Ill., 1963.
Operating Manual for Spaceship Earth, Carbondale, Ill., 1969.
Utopia or Oblivion. The Prospects for Humanity, New York, 1969.
The Buckminster Fuller Reader, edited by James Meller, London, 1970.
I seem to be a Verb, New York, 1970.
Buckminster Fuller to Children of Earth, edited by Cam Smith, Garden City, NY, 1972.
Intuition, New York, 1972, revised edition, Garden City, NY, 1973.
Earth Inc., Garden City, NY, 1973.
Synergetics. Explorations in the Geometry of Thinking, in collaboration with E.J. Applewhite, New York, London, 1975.
Tetrascroll. Goldilocks and the Three Bears. A Cosmic Fairytale (1975), New York, 1982.
And It Came to Pass – Not to Stay. New York, London, 1976.
Synergetics 2. Exploration in the Geometry of Thinking, in collaboration with E.J. Applewhite, New York, London, 1979.
Buckminster Fuller Sketchbook, Philadelphia, PA, 1981.
Critical Path, New York, 1981, London, 1983.
Inventions: The Patented Works of R. Buckminster Fuller, St. Martin's Press, New York, 1983.
Humans in Universe (with Anwar Dil), New York, 1983.
Grunch of Giants, New York, 1983.
Cosmography. A Posthumous Scenario for the Future of Humanity, (with Kiyoshi Kuromiya) New York, 1992.